£5

THE GUINNESS & MAHON
GUIDE TO PENSIONS FOR INDIVIDUALS

The Guinness & Mahon Guide to Pensions for Individuals

Gill and Macmillan

Published in Ireland by
Gill and Macmillan Ltd
Goldenbridge
Dublin 8
with associated companies in
Auckland, Dallas, Delhi, Hong Kong,
Johannesburg, Lagos, London, Manzini,
Melbourne, Nairobi, New York, Singapore,
Tokyo, Washington

7171 1425 2
Print origination by
Printset & Design Ltd
Printed by Criterion Press, Dublin.

Contents

Introduction

Within the last sixty years, life expectancy at birth has increased from 47 years to approximately 72 years. The developments in medical science and social conditions which have led to this improvement have also led to enhanced life expectancy post retirement. For example, a male retiring today at age 65 can look forward to a life expectancy of another fifteen to seventeen years. For a female, there is an average expectancy of a further eighteen to twenty years active life.

Until they retire, people who have been working most of their adult years are usually unaware of how much their jobs and their work environments mean to them. Unprepared, many of them experience a tremendous sense of loss, emptiness and despair. To combat this, pre-retirement courses are now becoming increasingly popular to help employees make the transition from organisation life to private life. The purpose of such courses is to advise impending retirees on developing their personal interests, including development of hobbies, and awareness of the need to enhance their level of personal care. However, there is an increasing need to analyse financial requirements and the sources of retirement income.

The task of providing retirement income today falls on:

(1) The individual's ability to accumulate a retirement fund during working years.

(2) Government Retirement and Pensions programmes.

(3) Employer-Provided Retirement Plans.

People frequently receive retirement benefits from all these sources. In fact, it seems prudent not to rely entirely on only one or even two of these sources. A balance or diversification of retirement income sources seems best in most cases.

For a considerable period throughout our social and economic development, it was generally thought that the problem of providing for an old age income should be solved by the individual. However, in today's economy, with high taxes and recurrent inflation, the problem of amassing an adequate capital sum out of ones earnings is indeed a difficult one. Still, many people accumulate an investment fund during their working years to help provide for their retirement.

The second approach to the problem of financing old age security is from Government sponsored Retirement Plans. Because of the difficulties many people face in accumulating funds by direct savings, the Government has found it both economically desirable and politically expedient to provide State Pension Benefits. It is generally felt that the essential purpose of State Pensions is to provide a guaranteed income base, upon which the individual can build from his own resources.

The third method of handling the problem of retirement financing is for the employer to assume some of the burden. Company sponsored Pension Schemes have now become extremely important, and it is estimated that upwards of 50% of the working population are covered by some form of Company Pension Scheme.

Because of the complexity of the basic problem itself, and the enormous diversity of legal, social, and educational ramifications surrounding it, we have written this book as a definitive guide to Pensions for the Individual.

We believe that the information contained herein will be of enormous benefit to those already making some provisions for their Pensions, and it could be even more highly significant for those who have not as yet begun to plan for their retirement years.

I — Pensions for the Self-Employed

The self-employed are the most vulnerable group of people when it comes to providing for a Pension in retirement.

People like Doctors, Dentists, Solicitors, Accountants, Shopkeepers, Sole-Traders etc., depend entirely on their own efforts to provide an income during their working lifetime. Likewise, they must look to their own efforts to provide an income in retirement.

If you are self-employed, then you will know only too well that you have no Company Pension to look forward to while you are almost certainly not covered by the Social Welfare Pension Schemes either.

You must make your own arrangements.

1. THE SELF-EMPLOYED

1.1 INTRODUCTION

In this section we deal mainly with Pension, Life Assurance, and Disability Insurance Plans available to the "self-employed".

By "self-employed" we mean people who have a source of earnings assessible to income tax under either Schedule D Case I or 2 (that is income in respect of a trade or profession). This heading would cover people like sole traders, shopkeepers, doctors, dentists, farmers, solicitors and accountants. The term "self-employed" in this section can also be taken to include employees who are deemed to be in "non-pensionable" employment — in other words, employees working for a Company which does not operate any type of Pension Scheme for its employees.

People who run their business through a private company might look on themselves as being "self-employed". However, for Pension purposes, there is a fundamental difference beween someone who trades as a sole trader and someone who operates his business through a Company. Company Directors are covered in Chapter 6 of this book under the heading of Employees. As will be seen in Chapter 6, it is far more attractive to use your

Company, if you can, as the vehicle to provide your Pension than trying to achieve this as a "self-employed" individual.

It may be that you have a few different sources of income — one which might be assessible to tax under schedule D Case 1 or 2. In that case, this section of the book would apply in respect of that income while if you were also, for example, a full-time working Director of another company, Chapter 6 of this book would apply in respect of that source of income.

In this section, we deal with three separate areas:-

(1) Retirement Annuities:
These are a means of providing an income in retirement.

(2) Dependants' Benefits:
This includes Life Assurance protection for the benefit of your dependants.

(3) Disability Insurance:
This deals with providing an income should you be unable to work for a prolonged period due to sickness or disability.

2. RETIREMENT ANNUITIES

2.1 WHAT IS A RETIREMENT ANNUITY?

A Retirement Annuity is a special savings plan, normally operated by the Life Assurance Companies, to which self-employed people can contribute and build up a fund which can be used to provide a Pension in retirement. It is a particularly attractive way of providing for a pension because:

(1) All contributions to the Plan, up to certain limits, are fully tax-deductible, and

(2) The Fund into which the contributions are invested does not pay any tax on its investment profits.

Retirement Annuities were introduced originally in 1958. The Government of the day recognised the special position in which the self-employed find themselves with regard to providing for retirement. As will be seen in the Social Insurance section of this book, the self-employed are not covered by the Social Insurance Schemes. They must therefore provide for their own retirement and the Government felt that special tax concessions should be introduced to encourage people to make that provision.

To benefit from the attractive tax concessions (which will be discussed in more detail later), you must contribute to an "Approved" Retirement Annuity Contract. The legislation dealing with retirement annuities is found in section 235 of the 1967 Income Tax Act.

The major restrictions which the Revenue Commissioners have laid down with regard to retirement annuities are as follows:-

(1) The pension must normally not be payable before age 60 and not after age 70. In between these two ages, you may draw your pension at any stage. It is not necessary to stop working — you can start to draw your pension and continue working.

(2) A pension can become payable before age 60 if an individual becomes "permanently incapable through infirmity of mind or body of carrying on his own occupation or any occupation of a similar nature for which he is trained or fitted". In other words, you may draw on your pension before age 60 if you become seriously ill and unable to work. The Revenue Commissioners will also allow an individual to draw on his pension before age 60 if it is customary for people in that occupation to retire early.

(3) One quarter of the pension may be commuted at the time of payment for a tax free lump sum.

(4) A pension may also be provided after your death for the benefit of a spouse, or dependant. The stipulation is that the amount of the dependant's pension should not be greater than the amount payable to you during your lifetime.

(5) A pension, when it becomes payable, may be payable for a certain minimum period of time. In other words, the pension can provide for payment for a minimum period of at least, say, ten years regardless of whether you survive for that period or not. If you died before the end of the ten-year period, the balance of the pension payments would be made to your Estate. The maximum period for which the pension can be guaranteed to be payable is ten years.

Retirement Annuities are issued by Life Assurance Companies and are often referred to as Personal Pension Plans.

2.2 WHO CAN TAKE OUT A RETIREMENT ANNUITY?

Because of the attractive tax concessions, restrictions are placed on who may take out these Plans. The basic requirement is that you should be assessible to tax in respect of earnings under either Schedule D Case 1 or 2 or should be assessible to tax in respect of an income arising from non-pensionable employment.

Non-pensionable employment means being an employee of a company which does not have a Pension Scheme. Being covered for the various Pension Benefits under the Social Insurance Schemes would *not* be treated as being in pensionable employment. A Company Pension Scheme providing only for a death benefit payable to your next of kin would *not* be treated as pensionable employment. There may be cases where your employer has a Pension Scheme in operation, but you are not included in it for pension benefits because:

(1) Your employer may have decided not to include you, or

(2) You may have decided not to join the Scheme, if membership of it is voluntary, or

(3) There may be a minimum service requirement to join the Scheme of, say, five years and you have not yet completed that period of service.

In either of these cases you would be eligible to take out a Retirement Annuity currently as you are deemed to be in non-pensionable employment. If you subsequently join the Pension Scheme, you must stop contributing to your Retirement Annuity.

You may have more than one source of earnings and could be entitled to contribute to a Retirement Annuity in respect of one of those sources which might fall under Schedule D Case 1 or 2. Schedule D Case 1 or 2 refers to income arising from a trade or profession, respectively.

A husband and wife are treated separately for the purposes of retirement annuities. For example, if you were working in a company which had a Pension Scheme, then you would not be eligible to take out a Retirement Annuity. However, if your wife also had a source of income assessible to tax under Schedule D

Case 1 or 2 — for example, running a small business such as a shop or a hairdresser — then she would be entitled to take out a Retirement Annuity in respect of her source of income even though both of you may be taxed as one unit for income tax purposes.

2.3 DIFFERENT TYPES OF RETIREMENT ANNUITIES

There are many different types of Retirement Annuities currently available. However, all of these Plans can be distinguished by the following three factors:-

(1) Frequency of payment:
Under most Plans, you pay contributions on a regular basis for example on a monthly or half-yearly basis. However, there are also some Plans available where you can make a special once off contribution.

(2) Building up cash or pension:
Most Plans currently available are structured so as to build up a cash retirement fund. As pointed out previously, you are allowed to take one quarter of the total amount in the form of a tax free lump sum, generally referred to as "commuting" part of the pension, and the balance of the cash available must then be used to buy a pension at whatever rates are applicable at that stage. These type of Plans are often referred to as "funding for cash".

Let us say, for example, that you had been contributing to a Retirement Annuity for a number of years. You had just reached your 65th birthday and you had decided to draw down your benefits. The accumulated value of your Retirement Annuity is assumed to be £100,000.

Your options are:

(1) Pension Only:
You could take all of the benefits in the form of a pension. In that case, the £100,000 would be used to buy a pension which on *current* (August, 1985) annuity rates would probably give you a level pension for life of approximately £14,150 p.a.

OR

(2) Cash Lump Sum + Reduced Pension:
Take ¼ of the accumulated fund, i.e. £25,000, as a tax-free

lump sum and buy a pension with the balance of the fund, i.e. £75,000, to give a level pension for life of approximately £10,613 p.a., again based on *current* annuity rates.

On the other hand, most of the Plans available in the past were structured so as to build up a total pension payable on retirement. Again, an individual could commute a quarter of this pension for a tax free lump sum. This type of Plan was referred to as "Funding for Pension". There are very few "Funding for Pension" Plans currently available.

Where a Plan is funding for cash, you are carrying an additional investment risk in that you will not know until the moment of retirement what your precise pension will be as it will depend entirely on annuity or pension rates ruling at that time. Annuity rates offered by Life Offices vary in line with the level of interest rates available on Government Securities at that time. Therefore, with a Plan which is funding for cash, the timing of taking your benefits is crucial in that you will obviously want to retire at a time when you can buy the maximum possible level of pension, after taking your tax free lump sum.

With funding for pension Plans, on the other hand, the level of pension guaranteed is usually very low, as the Life Company involved is effectively estimating what annuity rates would be in 10, 20 or indeed 30 years time.

Many Plans might appear to be funding for pension in that the Policy Document might show a certain level of pension. However, these Plans are effectively funding for cash in that the pension stated is often a minimum guaranteed amount but the actual pension payable will normally be much higher if annuity rates at that stage are higher than the minimum guaranteed rate.

(3) Investment return:

As pointed out previously, a Retirement Annuity is simply a special Savings Policy to which you contribute in order to build up an income in retirement. Therefore, the investment return which you obtain from the Plan is the most important factor involved.

For example, £1,000 p.a. invested over 20 years would build-up the following accumulated fund based on different assumed investment returns:

At 8% p.a	:	£49,423
At 10% p.a.	:	£63,002 (+27%)
At 12% p.a.	:	£80,698 (+28%)

Therefore, an extra 2% p.a. return — from 8% to 10% p.a. — increases the accumulated fund by 27%.

All Retirement Annuities are not the same and as far as providing an investment return to the individual, they can be divided into three separate categories:-

(a) Unit-Linked.
(b) With Profit Endowment.
(c) Deposit Account.

Each of these three methods is discussed in turn below. However, at this point it should be pointed out that one of the tax advantages, referred to previously, of a Retirement Annuity is that funds invested with a Life Assurance Company under such a Plan will accumulate in the Life Assurance Company's hands completely free of income tax and capital gains tax. Therefore, your contribution can effectively be invested, to obtain a tax-free return. Neither yourself or the Life Assurance Company have any tax liability in respect of the investment return, regardless of which of the three types of Plans is used.

2.4 HOW UNIT-LINKED RETIREMENT ANNUITIES WORK

A Unit-Linked Retirement Annuity does not provide any guaranteed level of investment return. On the other hand, it offers a potentially higher return, albeit with a higher degree of risk, than either of the other two types. We look at how Unit-Linked Retirement Annuities work under the following headings:

— Unit Funds.
— Switching.
— Multi-Policy feature.
— Charges.
— Investment performance.
— Funding for Cash.
— Projected values.

Unit Funds:
Contributions to the Plan are used to purchase units in the chosen

Unit Fund. These Unit Funds operate along similar lines to Unit Trusts. The Fund is divided into units of equal value which are re-valued every week, or in some cases every month, upwards or downwards in line with the fluctuating value of the underlying investments. If you were, for example, contributing to a Plan on a monthly basis, then your contribution each month would purchase units at the price ruling that month. All investment income and capital gains or losses are fully reflected in the value of the units. Some Plans offer a choice of Funds into which you can invest your contribution. The most common choice is a Managed or Mixed Fund.

Managed Fund would invest in a mixture of Properties, Equities, Gilts and short term Deposits. Managed Funds are popular because people feel that the unit values are less likely to fluctuate due to the wide spread of assets contained in the Fund. With a Managed Fund, you are relying on the investment expertise of the Life Assurance Company to choose, from time to time, how much should be invested in each of the different investment sectors. They, as Professional Investment Managers, should know better than the layman when to alter the "mix" of the Managed Fund. Other choices of Funds would be Property, Equity, Gilt and Cash Funds.

Switching:

Where a choice of Funds is offered on a particular Plan, there is usually a switching facility. This means that you are entitled to switch your choice of Fund at various stages throughout the term of the Plan. The most popular type of switch envisaged would be where an individual might switch from a Managed Fund to a Cash Fund with a view to stabilising the capital value of his accumulated fund. During the Plan, it is also possible to re-direct future contributions into a different Fund and maintain your present holding in the previous Fund. For example, in some Plans you could have contributed to the Managed Fund for five years and then direct that future contributions only would be invested in, say, a Cash Fund. In this way you could build up a "mix" of funds.

Therefore, at retirement part of your units would be held in the Managed Fund and part in the Cash Fund. A Cash Fund alternative is highly desirable in a Plan: at approaching retirement, people do not necessarily want the value of their accumulated Fund to be fluctuating widely in value.

The difficulty with switching is knowing when to switch and indeed when not to switch. Units in a Managed Fund are not guaranteed. In fact, most Life Assurance Companys' literature says: "Unit values can fall as well as rise". There may therefore be periods in which the value of units could fall. The danger is that an individual, without seeking professional advice, could switch the value of his Plan from a Managed Fund to a Cash Fund just before the investment markets stage a recovery. Therefore, the switching facility is a very valuable option, but can be dangerous if exercised too often and without proper professional advice.

Multi-Policy Feature:

Some Unit-Linked Plans offer the facility of splitting your contribution up into a multitude of smaller individual Policies. One Plan allows the total contribution to be split up into as many as twenty individual Policies.

There are two advantages put forward for splitting your contribution up into a number of smaller Policies:-

(i) Where there is a choice of Unit Funds, it may be possible to invest in a mix of Funds by choosing different Fund links for each of the smaller individual Policies. For example, you could choose to have 60% of your contribution going to a Managed Fund with 40% going to a Cash Fund.

(ii) The main advantage is that it enables you to take your retirement benefits in stages. For example, you could decide to take the benefits under one or two of the individual Policies each year to enable you to phase in your retirement income in line with your declining earnings. This facility is also useful if you wish to take part of your benefits at a time when unit prices are depressed due to depressed investment conditions. You could delay withdrawing the benefits from some of the individual Policies until such time as the investment markets recover and the unit values increase.

Charges:

A Life Assurance Company will incur certain costs in setting up and maintaining a Policy on its books. The Plan will therefore contain certain charges and deductions to cover these costs.

One of the advantages put forward originally for Unit-Linked type Plans was the fact that charges were supposed to be visible and immediately apparent, compared with With Profit Endowment type Plans, so that you could tell immediately how much of your contributions were actually being invested.

However, modern Unit-Linked Plans have evolved a very complicated system of charges so that it is not obvious to the individual effecting the Plan what the charges are. Most Unit-Linked Plans would contain some or all of the following charges:-

(i) In the case of a regular contribution Plan, a certain percentage of the contribution will be used to purchase units. For example, a particular Plan might state that 97% of all contributions are used to purchase units, the 3% reduction being a charge.

(ii) There might be a policy fee deducted from the contribution e.g. £20 p.a., before investment of the contributions.

(iii) There is usually a 5% spread between the offer price of units and the bid price. Units are purchased at the offer price and are sold back to the Life Company when benefits are being taken from the Plan at their bid price. The 5% spread is therefore effectively a 5% sales charge on the purchase of units.

(iv) There is usually an annual management charge levied against the value of the Fund. This management charge is normally in the region of ¾% to 1% per annum of the value of the fund and is usually levied monthly. The price of units, as published in the newspapers or quoted direct by the Life Company, will already reflect the deduction in respect of this management charge. If, therefore, the units in a certain Managed Fund increased in value by 13% over a year, the actual return achieved might well have been 14% but 1% would have been deducted by the Life Company as its management charge.

The important point to note about these management charges is that in some cases, the level is guaranteed or there is an upper limit to the amount which can be charged, while in many other plans, the amount charged is completely at the discretion of the Life Company. In recent years, it has become more popular to have open-ended management charges attaching to Unit Funds. A typical management charge currently would be ¾% per annum.

(v) Most of the expenses which a Life Company incurs in setting up a Plan occur in the first two years. It is therefore common to find that the first two years contributions of a Plan are used to purchase different types of units often called "capital" or "initial" units. Contributions after the first two years would normally be used to purchase the ordinary units.

These initial or capital units are often presented as having an *additional* management charge in the region of 3% to 4% per annum. The Plan might therefore be presented as having 100% of contributions used to purchase units throughout but in the first two years, the units purchased would be these special units. These special units are normally exchanged for normal units of equal value after a certain period of time — for example 18 years. If these special units are surrendered before they are exchanged for normal units, for example when you decide to take your retirement benefits, then there is usually a surrender penalty levied against them.

All of this complicated arrangement is identical to having a lower percentage of your first two years contributions invested in normal units. For example, one particular Plan has 100% of contributions invested in units throughout, but with the first two years contributions being used to purchase special units.

These special units carry an additional management charge of 4.05% per annum over the normal units. These special units are exchanged for normal units after eighteen years. This in fact is identical to having 48% of your contribution in the first year and 50% in the second year invested to purchase normal units.

Investment Performance:

How have these various Pension Unit Funds performed to date? The table overleaf sets out the average annual growth rate over various periods in respect of the Personal Pension Managed Funds, currently available.

The average annual growth rates shown above would not be the return enjoyed by the Policyholder over that period. This is due to the fact that the above growth rates would not allow for any percentage of your premium which is not used to purchase units,

Company	Average unit growth rate to 1.7.1985		
	1 year % p.a.	2 years % p.a.	3 years % p.a.
New Ireland	19.4	19.5	24.1
Life Association	22.6	17.9	—
Abbey Life	18.9	18.8	22.1
Canada Life	7.6	7.2	12.8
Irish Life	16.1	12.4	20.6
Friends' Prov.	18.3	—	—
Standard Life	18.3	—	—
Insurance Corporation	16.4	13.8	18.8

the bid/offer spread, and the additional management charge in respect of any special units, and any policy fee.

How will these Funds perform in the future? Obviously no one can predict what the particular growth rate of any Fund will be in the future as this will depend on investment conditions in the future and on the skill of the Investment Managers involved.

Chosing a Unit-Linked Retirement Annuity solely on the basis of past performance can be dangerous due to the fact that this performance may not necessarily be reproduced in the future in any event, and also due to the fact that past performance tables as shown above do not take account of the differing charges and deductions applying to the various Plans.

Funding for Cash:

All the Unit-Linked Plans are of the type which are designed to provide a total cash fund at retirement from which you can then take one-quarter in the form of a tax free lump sum with the remaining three-quarters being used to purchase a pension based on annuity rates prevailing at that time. You are therefore carrying two investments risks:

(i) The risk attaching to the future growth rate of units in the chosen Fund.

(ii) The risk attaching to the annuity rates available at the time when you decide to take your retirement benefits. The conventional argument used to be that if unit values fell shortly before retirement this would almost certainly be accompanied by a rise in interest rates. If this happened, then annuity rates would almost certainly increase as well so that as far as the Pension part of the Plan was concerned, the fall in unit values might well be compensated by an increase in the annuity rates so that the same level of pension could be bought with a lower amount of money. However, experience in the recent past does not seem to fully bear out that point of view as the following graph shows:-

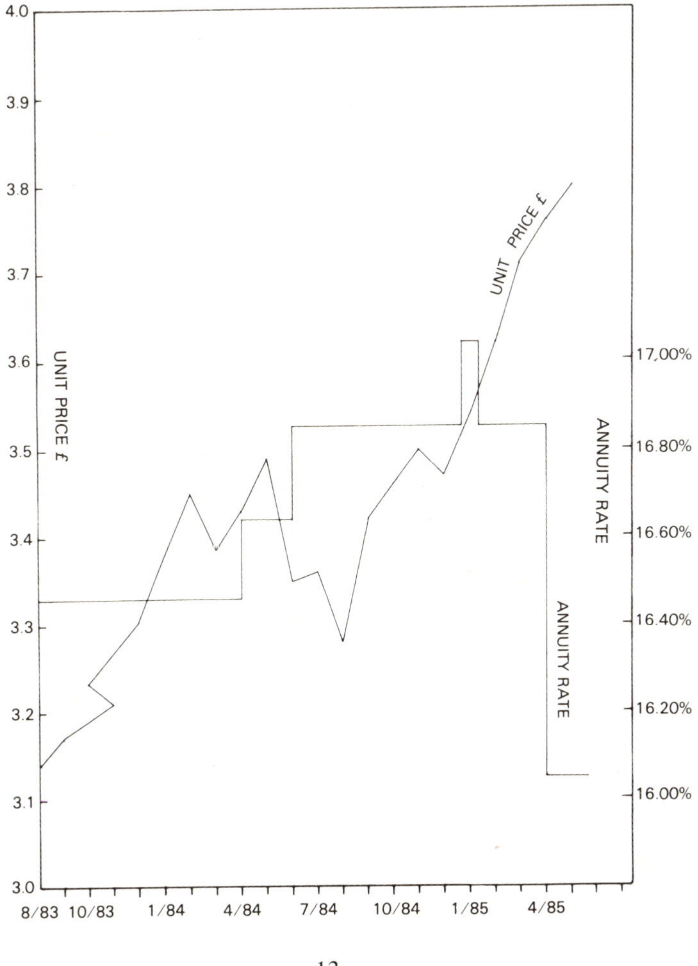

This graph shows the fluctuating value of a unit of the Irish Life Exempt Managed Fund from August, 1983 to May, 1985 compared with the Irish Life annuity rate for somebody retiring at age 65 at any stage throughout the same period. The annuity rate is expressed as the amount of pension p.a. which can be bought by £100. For example, an annuity rate of £16.50% means that for every £100 the Life Assurance Company would guarantee a level pension of £16.50 p.a. for life.

The graph shows that the annuity rate tended to change much less frequently than the price of the units. Therefore, choosing the right time to take your benefits under a Unit-Linked Retirement annuity is crucial.

Let us assume, for example, that you had been contributing to a Unit-Linked Retirement Annuity with Irish Life and by August, 1983 you had an accumulated fund of 50,000 units. If you stopped contributing then, then this table shows the value of your benefits assuming you delay taking your benefits until the dates shown:

				Retirement benefits	
Retirement Date	No. of units	Unit price* £	Annuity rate* £%	Tax free lump sum £	Pension for life £
1/8/83	50,000	2.986	16.45	37,325	18,419
1/5/84	50,000	3.312	16.65	41,400	20,680
1/8/84	50,000	3.116	16.85	38,950	19,689
1/1/85	50,000	3.362	17.05	42,025	21,495
1/5/85	50,000	3.613	16.05	45,163	21,745

*Unit price is the Bid Price of the Irish Life Exempt Managed Fund while the Annuity Rate is the Irish Life compulsory rate for a male aged 65, payable monthly in advance and guaranteed 5 years.

The difference in benefits between 1/1/85 and 1/5/85 is striking. While the tax-free lump sum is 7½% greater at 1/5/85, the pension is only 1% greater because the annuity rate had fallen in the meantime.

Projected Values:

An individual who is contemplating taking out a Unit-Linked Retirement Annuity will almost certainly be presented with a quotation or illustrated value of what the projected maturity value of the Plan will be in respect of a certain level of contribution. Most of these quotations are currently based on an *assumed* unit growth rate of 13% per annum and on certain stated annuity rates which are usually quite close to annuity rates which are currently prevailing. The whole question of projections and quotations is dealt with later on.

2.5 HOW WITH PROFIT RETIREMENT ANNUITIES WORK

A With Profit Retirement Annuity is very similar in design to the traditional With Profit Endowment type Life Assurance Policy. In other words, there is usually a certain basic sum guaranteed at maturity to which are added regular bonuses throughout the period of the Plan. With Profit Retirement Annuities are usually looked on as being less risky than Unit-Linked, containing minimum guaranteed returns, and potentially offering a lower return than Unit-Linked due to the lower degree of risk being accepted by the individual.

We look at how With Profit Retirement Annuities work under the following headings:

— Funding for Cash.
— Guarantees.
— Bonus Rates.
— Charges.
— Switching.
— Investment return.

Funding for Cash:

Most Plans are designed to provide a cash fund at the selected retirement age. Therefore, bonus rates are applied to a guaranteed minimum cash sum at retirement.

Guarantees:

One of the essential features which differentiates With Profit from Unit-Linked is the presence of some form of minimum guaranteed investment return. Typically, a Plan will have a prospective minimum guaranteed retirement fund in respect of a given level of contribution.

For example, one Plan guarantees for a male aged 45 next

birthday at the start of the Plan that in return for a contribution of £1,000 per annum, there will be a guaranteed minimum fund at age 65 of £27,597, assuming 21 annual premiums of £1,000 each are paid to that date. This works out at an effective minimum guaranteed rate of return of approximately 2.5% per annum. This guaranteed return is of course net of all charges and deductions. However, it could be argued of course that this type of minimum guaranteed return may be of little or no use in a period of high inflation.

Bonus Rates:

Investment profits, over and above those needed by the Life Assurance Company to meet the minimum guaranteed return, are added to your Plan by way of regular bonus additions to the basic guaranteed sum. There are usually two types of bonus additions:-

(i) *Reversionary Bonus:*

This is the annual bonus declared each year. A reversionary bonus can either be compound or simple, depending on whether the bonus is applied to the guaranteed sum plus attaching bonuses or simply to the original guaranteed sum, excluding attaching bonuses. A bonus might be declared for example at 6% compound, in which case the guaranteed sum plus attaching bonuses at that date would be increased by 6%.

A reversionary bonus is declared by the Life Assurance Company after its regular valuation by its Actuary. The bonus is basically a distribution of profits to the With Profit Policyholders in recognition of the extra investment return which the Company have obtained over and above the guaranteed return promised and the various expenses and deductions. The trend since the second world war has been for increasing levels of reversionary bonus to be declared. However, the important point to remember is that future bonus levels are *not* guaranteed. It is tempting to assume that the current rate of bonus being declared by the Life Company would at least continue to be paid in the future. However, there is increasing speculation, particularly in the U.K., that should interest rates fall to a lower level on a permanent basis, that Life Companies would have some difficulty in maintaining the current level of bonus rate.

However, on the other hand, it should be pointed out that Actuaries like to declare a bonus rate which they feel confident that they will be able to maintain in the future. There is therefore a ''smoothing-out'' of investment profits and losses from year to year in order to try to maintain a stable bonus rate.

(ii) *Terminal Bonus:*
This type of bonus has been introduced within the last decade and is a special bonus payable at the time the Policy matures — which in the case of a Retirement Annuity, would be at the date the benefits are drawn down. The terminal bonus is usually expressed as a percentage of attaching reversionary bonuses and is meant to reflect the capital profits which the Company has earned on its With Profit Funds. The terminal bonus rate is therefore likely to fluctuate much more so than the reversionary bonus. An example of a terminal bonus which one Company is currently paying on maturing policies is a rate of 45% of attaching reversionary bonuses. Therefore, in some cases the terminal bonus could account for a substantial portion of the retirement benefits.

The main distinction between a reversionary bonus and the terminal bonus is that once a reversionary bonus is declared, it is added to the guaranteed sum plus previously attaching bonuses and thereafter becomes guaranteed to be payable on retirement and cannot be withdrawn.

On the other hand, a terminal bonus only applies to policies maturing in the present year.

Take for example a particular Plan where for an individual aged 45 next birthday a guaranteed sum of £27,597 would be available at retirement at age 65 in respect of a level contribution of £1,000 per annum up to that date. Let us assume in this example that the bonus rate is currently 6.0% per annum compound. Therefore, the build up of the guaranteed sum, plus reversionary bonuses might look like those in the table overleaf:-

At the end of the first year the bonus of 6% is applied to the guaranteed cash fund at that stage of £27,597 to give a bonus addition of £1,655.82. This is then added to the cash fund so that the guaranteed figure at the end of the first year amounts to £29,252.82.

Guaranteed Cash Fund................	£27,597.00
Year 1	
Bonus at 6% on £27,597.............	£ 1,655.82
Guaranteed Cash Fund at retirement at end of year 1...........	£29,252.82
Year 2	
Guaranteed Cash Fund................	£29,252.82
Bonus at 6% on £29,252.82.........	£ 1,755.17
Guaranteed Cash Fund at retirement at end of year 2...........	£31,007.99

In the second year, the bonus of 6% is applied to this amount to give a new guaranteed figure at the end of the year of £31,007.99.

Therefore, although the *future* level of reversionary bonus is not guaranteed, when a bonus is actually declared, it is then added on and becomes guaranteed and may not be withdrawn in the future. On the other hand, the terminal bonus rate currently payable this year is of no consequence to an individual whose plan is not due to mature for another, say, ten years. The terminal bonus, if any, which applies in the year in which you draw your benefits will be the one that will apply to your Policy.

A potential criticism of the reversionary bonus method is that the Actuary in declaring the rate will always hold back some emerging profits so as to ensure that the rate can be continued in the future.

The bonus system is an averaging or pooling basis in which one bonus rate is declared for a whole category of Policies without necessarily taking account of the individual contribution to investment profits which any particular Policy would have made.

Charges:
Under the With Profits system charges are not explicit or visible as in the Unit-Linked system. The guaranteed minimum returns and the reversionary bonuses declared are net of expenses and

deductions. However, if you chose to draw your benefits earlier than the selected retirement age, there may well be a penalty or deduction made in respect of this early retirement. However, generally speaking, charges are not visible and are already taken into account when bonus rates etc., are declared. Therefore, one potential criticism of the With Profit system is that it is not possible to determine how much of your contribution is being taken off in expenses and how much is being invested.

Switching:
A few Companies offer both the Unit-Linked and With Profit versions of their retirement annuities. One or two Plans offer the prospect of starting off on the With Profit method and switching to the Unit-Linked method at some stage or vice versa. However, as pointed out for switching within the Unit-Linked Plans, the option to switch can be dangerous if not used with professional advice.

Investment Return:
The actual return achieved by a With Profit Plan will ultimately depend on the amount of guarantees, if any, the rate of reversionary bonus to be declared in the future, and the rate of terminal bonus, if any, which will be paid when benefits are drawn. The rate of bonus which may be declared by the Life Company, for example £6.00%, should not be confused with a rate of interest.

Page 20 shows an example of the types of prospective returns which two With Profit Plans from two different Companies are *currently* offering:-

The figures at (1) represent the guaranteed fund available at age 65 and the equivalent rate of return. (2) represents the guaranteed amount with reversionary bonus additions which are assumed will be payable in the future at the *current* rate of bonus declaration. (3) represents (2) with the additional terminal bonus, again assumed at the *current* rate payable. It should be pointed out at this stage that Plan B would, in the event of death before age 65, merely give a return of premiums paid without interest whereas Plan A would provide a return of premiums *with* accumulated interest. The returns on death under Retirement Annuities are considered later on in this chapter.

If we therefore assume that *current* rates of reversionary bonuses

Contribution of £1,000 P.A. for individual
aged 45 next birthday to age 65

	With profit plans Plan A	Plan B
(1) *Guaranteed Fund at 65*	£29,459	£27,597
Equivalent rate of return	3.0% p.a.	2.4% p.a.
(2) *Guaranteed Fund + Reversionary Bonus*	£87,579	£95,697
Equivalent rate of return	11.7% p.a.	12.3% p.a.
(3) *Guaranteed Fund + Reversionary Bonus + Terminal Bonuses*	£104,223	£107,563
Equivalent rate of return	13.0% p.a.	13.2% p.a.

will continue to be paid in the future, both Plans are giving a potential return in the region of 12% per annum with the addition of the terminal bonus adding approximately 1% per annum to this potential return.

2.6 HOW DEPOSIT ACCOUNT TYPE PLANS WORK

This type of Plan is often referred to as Deposit Account or Deposit Administration. They are closer to the With Profit method than they are to Unit-Linked. The Deposit Account type plan operates on a basis very similar to a Building Society or Bank Deposit. Contributions are paid each year and these contributions, less certain charges, are credited to your account. Each year, the Life Assurance Company declares a dividend or rate of interest for that year which is then applied to the balance of your account. We look at Deposit Account type Plans under the following headings:

— Funding for Cash.
— Dividends.
— Guarantees.
— Charges.
— Investment Return.

Funding for Cash:
All of these Plans operate on the basis of building up a cash fund to provide retirement benefits.

Dividends:
An essential feature of the Deposit Account type Plans is the declaration by the Life Assurance Company each year of a dividend or rate of interest. This dividend is applied to the balance in your account at that year. For example, in one such plan the dividend declared for 1984 was 15%. The dividend rate may vary from year to year and is more likely to fluctuate than the reversionary bonus under the With Profit type Plan. Nevertheless, the dividend rate does not fluctuate directly in line with general interest rates but moves on a more gradual basis either upwards or downwards in line with the longer-term trend in interest rates.

This table below shows by way of example the operation of the dividend rate:-

Deposit Account

(1)	Balance in account	:	£5,300
	Contribution for year	:	1,000
	Balance at year-end	:	£6,300
	Dividend rate	:	13%
	Dividend added to account is 13% x £6,300	:	£819
	Balance at year-end	:	£7,119
(2)	Balance in Account	:	£7,119
	Contribution for year	:	1,000
	Balance at year end	:	£8,119
	Dividend rate	:	12.5%
	Dividend added to account is 12.5% x £8,119	:	£1,014
	Balance at year-end	:	£9,133

(1) represents the transactions in a particular year where the opening balance in the account is £5,300 to which is added the

contribution for that year of £1,000. The dividend rate declared at the end of that year is taken at 13%, which is applied to the balance in the account at that stage to give a dividend amount for the year of £819.00 to give a total balance at the end of the year of £7,119. (2) represents the transactions in the following year when the dividend rate declared is slightly lower at 12.5%. The level of future dividend rates is *not* guaranteed.

Guarantees:
The Deposit Account type Plan usually carries the following guarantees:-

(i) The contributions credited to the account are completely secure and do not decrease in value, provided benefits are taken at the selected retirement age.

(ii) Dividends once added to the account cannot be taken away and are secure.

With some Plans if benefits are taken prior to the selected retirement age, there may be a penalty levied against the Fund in respect of the early retirement.

Charges:
The charges involved in a Deposit Account type Plan are usually more visible than in the With Profit version. Charges are often similar to those found in a Unit-Linked Plan:

(i) A certain percentage of the contribution is usually credited to the account. For example, in one Plan 95% of the regular contributions are credited to the account. The 5% represents the equivalent 5% bid/offer spread found in the Unit Funds under the Unit-Linked approach.

(ii) There may be an annual policy fee.

(iii) A lower rate of dividend is usually declared in respect of the contributions paid during the first two years. The reduction is usually in the region of 3% to 4% per annum so that if the normal dividend rate for the year was 13%, perhaps 9% would be the dividend rate applied to that part of the account represented by the first two years contributions. This type of structure is virtually identical to the special initial or capital units which were outlined earlier under the Unit-Linked version.

One particular Deposit Account type Plan specifies a reduction in the dividend rate of 3.6% per annum for that part of the account secured by the first two years contributions. This lower rate of dividend applies for a maximum of 24 years. As for the Unit-Linked type arrangement, this effectively means that there is 42% of the contribution invested in the first year and 44% in the second year.

(iv) There may also be a management charge specified which may be deducted *after* the declaration of the dividend rate. If therefore, a dividend of 13% is declared and the management charge was specified at ¾ % per annum, then effectively the dividend being declared is 12¼%.

Investment Return:
The investment return obtained by a policyholder will depend entirely on the future level of dividends. Some Plans specify a minimum guaranteed rate of dividend, before charges, while others specify no minimum at all, other than the guarantee that there will at least be the sum of the premiums paid available as a retirement fund. If we take the example of a Plan where the Life Assurance Company is *currently* declaring a dividend at the rate of 15% per annum, then the prospective investment returns would be as follows:-

Contribution of £1,000 P.A.
for individual aged 45 next birthday to age 65
Deposit Account Plan

Guaranteed Minimum Fund at 65	:	£37,262
Estimated Fund with dividends assumed at 12½% p.a.	:	£88,038
Equivalent rate of return	:	11.7% p.a.

The difference between the prospective rate of return of 11.7% per annum and the assumed dividend rate of 12½% per annum is accounted for by the various deductions in respect of the charges outlined previously.

A variation on the Deposit Account type plan already outlined is where each years contribution secures a guaranteed rate of dividend payable to retirement, based on interest rates ruling at the time the contribution is paid.

For example, a contribution being paid at the begining of 1985 might secure a guaranteed dividend rate of, say, 10.5% per annum from now to retirement age. As this dividend is credited to the account in future years, it in turn is reinvested and secures a guaranteed dividend rate based on interest rates ruling at that stage. This is often referred to as a "new money" approach, due to the fact that new contributions paid secure a different investment return than contributions already paid.

Unfortunately, the distinction between Unit-Linked, With Profit, and Deposit Account type arrangements are not as clear as they once were. For example, there is a With Profit Plan and a Deposit Account Plan, from different Life Companies, currently available on the market which are effectively run along Unit-Linked lines. In other words, the bonus rate or dividend rate is applied to units purchased by contributions. The Plan is still a With Profit or Deposit Account Plan but is presented as a Unit-Linked Plan.

As pointed out previously, many Plans now offer the right to switch between, say, Unit-Linked to With Profit or Deposit Account or vice versa.

2.7 WHAT HAPPENS ON DEATH BEFORE RETIREMENT?

If you should die before you draw your retirement benefits, most Plans provide for the payment of a lump sum to your Estate. Legislation demands that the lump sum is paid to your legal personal representatives and will then be distributed according to your Will, if you had made a Will, or according to the Succession Act, where you had not made a Will.

The amount of the lump sum payment on death will vary according to the type of Plan:-

(1) Unit-linked:

Under Unit-Linked Plans, the lump sum payment is usually the full encashment value of the units purchased by contributions up to the date of death. Therefore, in the earlier years, the amount of life cover will be little more than the premiums paid to date but will increase as the unit values, hopefully, increase in value.

The table below sets out the estimated lump sum payable on death under a particular Unit-Linked Plan, assuming that units grow in value at the rate of 13% per annum compound:

Estimated sum payable on death
for £1,000 P.A. Contribution

After	
5 Years	£ 6,408
10 Years	£17,841
15 Years	£38,787
20 Years	£77,459

(2) With profit plans:

The sum payable on death under a With Profit Plan varies according to the particular type of Plan. In some Plans there is no return on death at all, in others there is a return of contributions paid before death *without* interest, in others the return of contributions is *with* interest, while in some other Plans, there is a payment equal to the accumulated retirement fund, plus bonuses declared to date. The practice varies but the more common type of arrangement is for contributions to be refunded *without* interest. Under this type of Plan, your death, shortly before you intended to draw on your retirement benefits, can leave your next of kin much worse off than if you had drawn the retirement benefits shortly before death.

Taking for example a man aged 45 contributing £1,000 per annum to a With Profit Pension Plan which provides for a death benefit of return of contributions *without interest* on death. The projected retirement fund, allowing for *current* reversionary bonuses but ignoring terminal bonus, and the corresponding lump sum death benefit, assuming death occurs shortly before age 65, are as follows:-

Contribution of £1,000 P.A. to age 65
to with profit plan

Projected Retirement Fund at 65	£95,697
Death Benefit just before retirement	£21,000

There is therefore a sharp difference between the total value of benefits which can be obtained on retirement and the corresponding death benefit shortly before retirement. With such a Plan, it is therefore desirable to effect some additional Life Assurance cover to make up this potential shortfall.

(3) Deposit account:
Under the Deposit Account type Plan, there is usually a return of the fund or account, inclusive of dividends already declared, on death.

It is possible to effect additional Life Assurance protection in conjunction with their Retirement Annuities. This is covered in more detail in Chapter 3.

2.8 CAN YOU RETIRE EARLY BECAUSE OF ILL-HEALTH?
Yes. Normally you may not draw on your Retirement Annuity until age 60 at the earliest. However, legislation does provide for retirement early on grounds of ill-health where an individual has become "permanently incapable through infirmity of mind or body, of carrying on his own occupation or any occupation of a similar nature for which he is trained or fitted".

The important point in the legislation is the word "permanent". In other words, if you become ill but you are likely to recover and resume your business, then this would not be grounds under which you could draw on your Retirement Annuity Policy before age 60. What the legislation allows for is permanent disablement or illness, which is unlikely to be reversed.

2.9 INCOME TAX RELIEF:
One of the major attractions of a Retirement Annuity is the attractive income tax relief allowed on contributions paid.

Income tax relief is allowed on contributions paid to a Retirement Annuity in a tax year, up to a maximum level of 15% of "net relevant earnings" in that tax year. Relevant earnings would be your income assessible to tax in that year, arising from either Schedule D case I or 2 cr, from Schedule E in the case where you are in non-pensionable employment. Net relevant earnings are your relevant earnings reduced by certain allowable losses and capital allowances and other items such as mortgage interest.

The rules regarding income tax relief are as follows:-

(1) A contribution paid is allowed first of all against your income in that tax year up to 15% of net relevant earnings. A full contribution, up to the 15% limit, can be written off against tax so that the gross and net outlay for a contribution of £1,000 per annum would be as follows:-

Gross Contribution	Marginal Tax Rate	Tax Relief	Net Contribution
£	%	£	£
1,000	35	350	650
1,000	48	480	520
1,000	60	600	400

(2) Where more than 15% of net relevant earnings is paid in a particular tax year, then the excess may be carried forward into the following tax year in order to obtain relief and so on until relief is fully claimed.

(3) There is a provision whereby a contribution paid in a particular tax year may be, for income tax relief purposes, treated as having been paid in an earlier tax year. This is referred to as a "backdating" provision. A contribution may be backdated for income tax relief purposes to a particular year of assessment provided your assessment for that year has become "final and conclusive" — that is agreed with the Revenue — within the last six months.

Example:
We are now in the income tax year 1985/86. Normally, if you pay a contribution to a Retirement Annuity in this tax year, it will be allowed against your tax for 1985/86. If, however, your assessment for say, 1983/84 has become "final and conclusive" within the last six months, then any contribution which you pay now could, if you wished, be backdated to the tax year, 1983/84 and you could obtain relief against your tax payable for that year.

2.10 OTHER TAX CONCESSIONS:
In addition to the income tax relief a Retirement Annuity also carries two other valuable tax concessions:-

(1) The contributions invested with the Life Assurance Company

will accumulate free of income tax and capital gains tax. This is so because the Life Assurance Company is not taxed on that part of its funds represented by Retirement Annuity and Pension Fund investments.

(2) As pointed out previously, one quarter of the accumulated fund may be taken in the form of a tax-free lump sum. The balance of the fund must be used to buy a pension and this pension is treated as earned income and is liable to tax.

2.11 FLUCTUATING EARNINGS:

It is not uncommon to find that self-employed people have a fluctuating level of earnings. Unlike people in employment, your earnings may not increase regularly on a defined basis year by year. You may have a "good year" followed by a "bad year". If your earnings are likely to fluctuate in such a manner, then at first glance it might seem more sensible to effect a series of once-off contribution Retirement Annuities in line with the level of fluctuating earnings. A series of once off contribution Plans would normally offer better value for money than a regular contribution Plan due to the lower level of expenses involved, particularly for someone close to retirement.

However, there are reasons why a series of once off Plans may not necessarily be the best thing:

(1) A regular contribution plan does allow you to budget precisely for the regular outgo. For example, if you are contributing £200.00 a month to such a Plan, then this amount can be built in to your planned expenditure. On the other hand, if you were to pay on a once-off basis each year, it could well happen that the equivalent £2,400 might not be available on a regular annual basis out of funds. Income tax bills would also have to be paid in one lump sum and there would always be the temptation to delay contributing to a Retirement Annuity Plan until your financial situation improved. Therefore, the contractural nature of a regular contribution plan being paid by monthly direct debit, for example, does help to ensure that you keep up your saving programme.

(2) Where contributions are being made on a once off basis each year, it is very likely that you will be influenced by short term

past investment considerations when investing your contribution. For example, in a particular year when Unit-Linked Funds had not performed very well, it is likely that you might either delay investing your contribution at all or invest it in a With Profit or Deposit Account type Plan.

In the long term, such a decision based on short term factors may not necessarily be the best one. With once off contributions, timing also becomes vital in that, for example, if Unit-Linked Funds had performed exceptionally well recently, you may well invest a substantial lump sum at a time when unit prices are at a peak. With a regular contribution plan you are less likely to be influenced by such short term factors and, in the case of a Unit-Linked Plan, your contributions will be buying units on a regular basis, both when prices are high and when prices are low.

Nevertheless, once off contribution plans can be useful particularly for people approaching retirement. In the case of someone with fluctuating earnings a compromise might be to effect a regular contribution plan or plans at a certain level which it is envisaged you will be able to maintain regardless. Then in particularly good years, you could always top up this contribution by making a special once off contribution possibly to a different type of plan — for example, if your regular contribution plan was a With Profit one, then your once off contribution might be made to a Unit-Linked Plan, thereby spreading your investment risk. Many regular contribution plans now contain options whereby you can stop, skip, and start contributions again without penalty in certain circumstances. However, there may be penalties in stopping or skipping contributions in the very early years of the Plan.

2.12 WHAT HAPPENS IF YOU ARE NO LONGER SELF-EMPLOYED?

If you cease to be self-employed by, for example, forming a Company or by joining another Company and becoming an employee, then you may have to stop contributing to your Retirement Annuity Plan. You would have to stop contributing if your new employment was "pensionable". If your new employment, on the other hand, does not have any Company Pension Scheme, then you are entitled to continue contributing to your Retirement Annuity. If you form your own Company, then you obviously can decide whether or not your new Company will have a Pension Scheme. Invariably, it will be more attractive to have a Company Pension arrangement rather than maintain your own personal Retirement Annuity. This is covered in more detail in Chapter 6.

2.13 DRAWING ON YOUR RETIREMENT ANNUITY

As pointed out previously, you may draw on your Retirement Annuity at any stage after age 60, or earlier on grounds of serious ill-health. Your options with regard to benefits will normally be as follows:-

(1) You may use the full accumulated fund, in a case where the Plan was funding for cash, to purchase an annuity. This annuity or pension must be purchased with a Life Assurance Company, but since 1979 you are entitled to buy your annuity with whatever Life Office is offering the best rates at that time. Your are not restricted to buying your annuity with the Company with which your Retirement Annuity Plan was placed. However, some companies are not prepared to accept an ''incoming'' lump sum to purchase annuities so that your choice may not be as wide as you might think.

(2) As an alternative, you may take up to one-quarter of the accumulated fund in the form of a tax-free lump sum and buy an annuity with the balance. In any event, the annuity will be treated as taxable income and the Life Assurance Company paying the annuity will operate the P.A.Y.E. system in payment.

(3) The annuity can take many forms:-

(a) It may be *level or escalating*. For example, you could purchase an annuity which would increase each year at the rate of 5% per annum compound.

(b) The annuity could be payable monthly, quarterly, half-yearly or yearly, as desired.

(c) The annuity can be payable for life or for life but with a guaranteed minimum period of payment of at least, say, five or ten years. The ten year guaranteed period is the maximum allowed and this would provide that regardless of whether or not you survive the ten year period, the annuity would be payable for that ten years. If you died before the end of the period, the balance of the payments would be made to your Estate.

(d) You could buy an annuity whereby in the event of your death, the annuity or a portion of it would continue to be payable to your widow or widower or to some other dependant. You could buy an annuity, for example, which on your death would reduce to half of the original amount and would continue to be paid while that dependant lived.

Annuity rates are often expressed as the annual amount of pension purchased by £100. In other words, an annuity rate of £15.00% would mean that a payment of £100 would secure an annuity of £15.00 per annum for life.

Annuity rates will vary according to the following factors:

(a) The *level of interest rates* at the time the annuity is purchased. As an annuity is effectively an investment with a Life Assurance Company, the amount of income which the Company will guarantee to pay in return will depend on the type of investment return which they feel they can earn on the sum invested with them. Therefore, as interest rates rise, annuity rates will tend to rise in line because the life company will be able to obtain a high return. Conversely, if interest rates fall, then so will annuity rates. However, once an annuity is purchased with a Life Assurance Company, that rate is guaranteed to be payable for the rest of your life.

(b) *Your age.* Where an annuity is payable for life, the older you are at the time the annuity is purchased, then the higher the annuity rate will be. This is so because the older you are the shorter the remaining expectation of your life is. The Life Assurance Company can therefore afford to offer a better rate than for a younger life as they estimate the pension will be payable for a shorter period of time.

(c) *Whether the annuity is level or increasing.* Where an annuity is guaranteed to increase at, say, 5% per annum, then the Life Assurance Company will offer a lower initial annuity as they will have to increase this amount each year by 5% compound. An increasing annuity is more realistic than a level one, because experience shows that the cost of living does increase. Indeed, an increase of the rate of 5% per annum would not even be enough to keep pace with inflation currently. However, a level annuity does appear more attractive initially due to the higher level payable in the first year, compared with the increasing annuity.

(d) *Whether the annuity has a guaranteed minimum period of payment.* Again, a slightly lower annuity rate would apply in the case of an annuity that is guaranteed to be payable for, say, five or ten years compared with an annuity that ceases immediately on death.

(e) *How frequently the annuity is payable.* Where the annuity is payable annually, a slightly lower rate will be offered compared to an annuity which is payable monthly due to the fact that the Life Company have the use of the funds invested that little bit longer in the case of a monthly paid annuity.

(f) Whether there is *any provision for a dependants annuity.* If there is so, then the annuity rate will be lower than where such provision does not apply because the Life Assurance Company will estimate that it will have to pay this additional dependants annuity for a certain period after your death.

(g) *Sex.* Lower annuity rates apply to females than to males because they are likely to live longer than males of the same age. Statistics do show this and hence annuity rates reflect their higher expectation of life.

The table across illustrates many of the points above by setting out the *current* annuity rates which one Company is currently (August, 1985) offering to people retiring:

This example below shows how annuity rates are applied in practice.

Let us assume that you have reached age 60 and wish to take your retirement benefits. Your accumulated retirement fund is £100,000 under either a Unit-Linked or With Profit Plan. Assuming

Type of Pension		Annual income per £100 investment		
		Males		Females
		60	65	65
		£	£	£
(1)	*Basic Annuity*			
	No Guarantee	13.32	14.63	13.14
	Guaranteed*	12.48	13.15	12.40
(2)	*Basic Annuity*			
	Increasing at 5% p.a.*	8.76	9.87	8.64

*Annuities guaranteed payable for at least ten years. All Annuities payable monthly in advance.

that you wish to purchase a basic annuity for yourself, increasing at the rate of 5% per annum, then your options might be as follows:-

(1) *Full Annuity**:
£100,000 x 8.76% = £8,760 p.a.

OR

(2) *Tax-Free Lump Sum*:
£100,000 x ¼ =£25,000

PLUS

(3) *Reduced Annuity**:
£100,000 x ¾ x 8.76% =£ 6,570 p.a.

*Assumed to be payable monthly in advance, guaranteed period of 10 years and increasing at 5% p.a.

Some Plans carry a minimum guaranteed annuity rate. For example one With Profit Plan has a minimum guaranteed annuity rate at age 65 of 11.11%. Therefore, even if rates generally available in the market are lower than this at retirement, that Life Assurance Company will offer a rate at least equal to 11.11%. The guaranteed rate usually corresponds to an assumed rate of interest in the region of 6% per annum. If, therefore, you feel that interest rates at the time of your retirement might be less than 6%, then the guarantee would be of value to you. If, on the other hand, you feel that interest rates would be greater than 6% at retirement, then the guarantee is of no value.

2.14 LOAN BACKS AND PENSION MORTGAGES

One objection that was often put forward to the Retirement Annuity was the fact that, barring serious ill-health, your money was locked away until age 60 at the earliest. To counteract this objection, the "Loan-Back" facility has been introduced on some Retirement Annuity Plans within the last few years.

A Loan-Back is an arrangement whereby the Life Assurance Company is willing to lend back to you the value of your accumulated contributions in a Retirement Annuity. The legislation governing Retirement Annuities does not allow you to offer the Policy as security for the loan. Hence normal security must be offered for the loan. While the loan is outstanding you pay interest at a fluctuating rate in respect of the balance outstanding. Normally, full repayment of the loan is required when retirement benefits are taken from the Plan or on earlier death.

For Unit-Linked Plans offering this facility it is normal to find that if a loan is taken, then some or all of your units purchased at that stage are transferred to a special account which is credited with the same rate of interest, less certain deduction in charges, which you pay in the form of interest on the loan.

If the purpose of the borrowing is for business purposes, then it may be possible to claim full income tax relief on the interest paid.

Generally speaking, Loan-Backs should only be used for genuine borrowing purposes and then only for short periods if at all possible. The disadvantage of using the Loan-Back facility is that in the long run, the investment performance of your Plan will probably suffer. This is so because when you draw down a loan, the value of your Plan may be switched to a special basis, as already referred to, so that future growth in the value of your Plan would probably be related to the rate of interest which you are paying on the loan. Also remember that normal security must be offered for the loan and that the loan is repayable on retirement.

Of course, when you draw your retirement benefits you could, if the amount is sufficient, repay the loan out of the one-quarter tax-free lump sum which you may take.

A "Pension Mortgage" is a way of repaying a loan over a period of time through a Retirement Annuity. The concept is simple. You borrow money from the Life Assurance Company or other financial Institution. The target repayment date for the loan might be set at your 60th birthday. You pay interest on the whole loan outstanding until the loan is repaid in one lump sum on your 60th birthday.

The repayment of the loan is provided for by effecting a Retirement Annuity at such a level of contribution that on "conservative" investment assumptions the one-quarter tax-free lump sum on the retirement annuity would cover the amount of the loan to be repaid on your 60th birthday.

Again, the Retirement Annuity cannot be used as security so normal security must be provided for the loan. The Pension Mortgage is effectively a way of repaying your capital so as to obtain full income tax relief on capital repayments. The interest payments would qualify for income tax relief provided the money is borrowed for business reasons. The contribution to the Retirement Annuity would qualify for full income tax relief up to the 15% limit specified earlier. Of course, only people eligible to effect a Retirement Annuity can consider a Pension Mortgage.

This example shows the workings involved in a Pension Mortgage:-

Age Now:	40.
Amount Borrowed:	£50,000.
Interest Rate on loan:	19% p.a. (assumed)
Repayment at 60.	
Annual Interest Payment:	
19% x £50,000 =	£9,500 p.a.
Retirement Annuity:	
£3,276 p.a. contribution gives	
projected fund at 60:	£200,000
Tax-free lump sum (¼):	£ 50,000

The Retirement Annuity shown in this example is based on a Unit-Linked Plan and assumes a unit growth rate of 10% per annum. Therefore, a contribution of £3,276 per annum would give a total projected fund at 60 based on a 10% unit growth rate of almost £200,000 of which one-quarter would give £50,000. The tax-free lump sum could therefore be taken and the loan repaid in one amount. The balance of the accumulated fund must be used to buy a pension.

Provided the borrowing is for business purposes and the Retirement Annuity contribution is within the 15% limit each year, then the full interest and, effectively, capital repayments are offsettable against your marginal rate of tax. This of course is a very attractive proposition compared with the normal lending arrangement whereby only the interest payments would be tax deductible.

However, the Pension Mortgage does carry some disadvantages and risks in some cases:

(1) If for some reason you need to repay the mortgage before age 60 then you *cannot* draw on your Retirement Annuity funds. If, in our example above, the individual aged 40 wished to repay the loan ten years later at age 50 he would have to find the funds elsewhere as he would not be able to get his tax-free lump sum from his Retirement Annuity until age 60 at the earliest, except in the case of serious ill-health.

(2) Depending on the type of Retirement Annuity used to provide the funds to repay the loan, there may be an element of risk involved. If, for example a Unit-Linked Plan is used, then the recommended contribution rate is calculated on an *assumed* unit growth rate — in our example above, this was taken at 10% per annum. If the chosen Unit Fund does not achieve this growth rate, then insufficient funds will be available to repay the loan fully.

(3) The tax-free lump sum is, in most cases, being earmarked for the repayment of part or all of the loan. It should therefore be realised that one of the attractive advantages of the Retirement Annuity is being given up.

Nevetheless, for some people, the disadvantages and risks outlined above may not be material and their circumstances will make such a Pension Mortgage route an attractive means of borrowing money.

2.15 GROUP RETIREMENT ANNUITIES:

Up to now, we have been dealing entirely with *individual* Retirement Annuities, which any individual, entitled to do so, could effect. However, the legislation does provide for individuals "engaged in or connected with a particular occupation" to club together and join in a Group Scheme under one Retirement Annuity.

Some of the professions and groups which have set up these Schemes include Doctors, Farmers, Solicitors and Accountants. In many cases, the Group Retirement Annuity, to which members of the association or profession can contribute to, is very similar in design to the various individual Retirement Annuities which we have covered above.

However, in some limited cases, the profession or association have set up their own private Investment Fund which is not linked with any Life Assurance Company. The advantage in joining a Group Retirement Annuity arrangement with a Life Assurance Company as opposed to effecting an individual one is that the Life Assurance Company usually makes slightly lower expense deductions on the group arrangement than on the individual arrangements. On the other hand, the profession or association setting up the group arrangement usually tends to have just one or maybe two Retirement Annuities with one Life Assurance Company. On the group arrangement, therefore, the individual may not have the same choice of plans open to him as an individual investor.

2.16 PROJECTED BENEFITS

It is natural that if you are considering contributing to a Retirement Annuity, you will wish to have some idea of the benefits which are likely to be obtained from that Plan. This desire has given rise to the practice of showing projected benefits at retirement in return for a given contribution.

The important point to realise about these projections is that they are *not guaranteed* benefits. The projections are based on several sets of assumptions, which if borne out in practice would result in the benefits shown being paid but if the assumptions are not borne out, then the actual benefits payable would be different from those illustrated. It is important to appreciate the assumptions underlying these projections. An example of this type of projection would be the following, which has been taken from an advertisement which appeared in the daily papers in the early months of 1985.

The advertisement shows that in return for a contribution of £1,000 per annum to age 65, you could expect the following benefits at retirement at age 65:

Pension per annum	:	£ 71,265
Plus tax-free lump sum	:	£148,470

These figures are in the "telephone" number bracket. Let us look behind these particular figures to see what assumptions are being made:-

Assumed Age:
The figures are in fact based on a male aged 30 next birthday, starting a Retirement Annuity Plan now and paying 36 annual contributions of £1,000 between now and age 65. This is really an unrepresentative age as many people naturally only start thinking about pensions in their middle to late forties.

Assumed Unit Growth Rate:
The particular Plan illustrated is a Unit-Linked Plan and the projections are based on an assumed unit growth rate of 13% per annum.

As pointed out previously, the essence of Unit-Linked Retirement Annuities is that there is no guaranteed return. Therefore, the 13% unit growth rate is an assumption which may or may not be borne out in practice.

The 13% rate assumed would be *after* the annual management charge so that in fact the Life Assurance Company would have to achieve an annual return of at least 13.75% per annum to meet the assumed 13% rate.

The 13% rate would be *before* the various other charges outlined previously that usually apply to Unit-Linked Plans. Because of these charges, even if the unit growth rate was to be 13% per annum throughout, the individual would not actually receive a return of 13% on his money but something, in this example, in the region of 12.3%. The difference represents the reduction in respect of the various charges involved.

While the unit growth rate assumption of 13% per annum may seem conservative, compared with the past performance of some of these Unit-Linked Funds, it should be remembered that the past returns have been produced in a period of high inflation and over a relatively short period of time. With inflation stabilising at lower levels, a future assumed unit growth rate of 13% p.a. may not be all that "conservative".

Projected Pension:

The projected Pension of £71,265 per annum is based on an *assumed* annuity rate of 16.00%. The *current* (August, 1985) annuity rate for a male retiring at age 65, assumed to be guaranteed for 5 years is £14.15%.

An annuity rate of 16.00% for somebody aged 65 implies that long term interest rates at retirement will be in the region of 13% to 14% per annum, as they are at present. In this particular example, the period to retirement will be 36 years. Is it reasonable, therefore, to assume that those types of long-term interest rates will be available in 36 years time?

Therefore, even if the average unit growth rate was to be 13% per annum, the tax-free lump sum would be as projected but the Pension may or may not be as projected, depending on annuity rates at that time.

The projected Pension figure of £71,265 per annum assumes that it will be a *level* Pension. The concept of a Pension which remains level in monetary terms throughout retirement is not really realistic. If you allow for inflation, this effectively means that the real value of your Pension will be declining, the longer you live. Furthermore, if you are assuming that annuity rates at the time of retirement will be based on interest rates in the region of 13% or 14% p.a., then presumably inflation could be in the region of 8% or 9%. A person retiring at age 65 could probably expect, on average, to live at least another seventeen years. Inflation at even modest levels could seriously erode the purchasing power of a level pension throughout this period. For example, this table shows the "real" or purchasing power value of a pension of £1,000 per annum starting now, in five and ten years time, allowing for inflation at different rates throughout:

Assumed inflation rate	Purchasing power in 5 years time	Purchasing power in 10 years time
%	£	£
5	783	614
7.5	696	485
10	621	385

Therefore, even with an inflation rate of just 5% per annum, a level pension would have lost approximately one-quarter of its purchasing power after five years and would have lost 40% of its value after ten years.

Therefore, it might have been more realistic to show a projected pension which would increase during payment. If the projected pension was to increase at the rate of 5% per annum compound, then the projected pension, on the same annuity rate assumptions, would have been reduced from the figure of £71,265 per annum to approximatley £56,000 per annum.

The projected Pension shown does not allow for any continuing payment to your spouse after death. If, for example, one half of the Pension would continue to be paid to your spouse after death then the projected Pension figure would have been reduced by approximately 5% to 6%.

What About Inflation?:

Probably the most serious objection to the projected figures as presented is the absence of any allowance for inflation. A Pension of £71,000 per annum seems an astronomical amount but what will it really be worth in 36 years time?

If we were to allow for inflation at the rate of 10% per annum between now and retirement — an assumption which might be consistent with assuming a gross investment return of 13.75% per annum — then the projected figures, when translated to todays money values, would look completely different:-

Benefit	Projected value	Projected values in todays terms
	£	£
Pension	71,265	2,305
Tax-Free Lump Sum	148,470	4,803

Of course, no one can predict what the average inflation rate over the 36 years will be or indeed what the average unit growth rate will be either. However, the adjusted figures shown above do show that the projected benefits, not adjusted for inflation in the intervening period can give a highly misleading picture.

One of the reasons why the benefits, adjusted for an assumed inflation rate of 10% per annum, appears so low is that the amount being contributed to the Plan is also, in ‘‘real’’ terms, declining year by year. Projected benefits are based on a *level* contribution to the Plan of £1,000 per annum. This diagram below shows the declining real value of a level annual contribution of £1,000, allowing for inflation at the rate of 10% p.a.

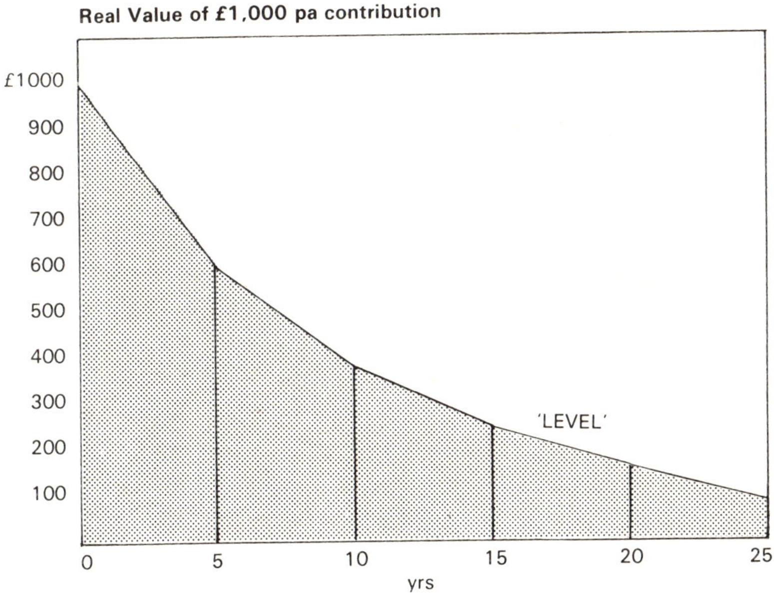

As pointed out in the next paragraph, you should really think in terms of contributing a certain percentage of your earnings to a Plan rather than a fixed monetary amount.

Projected benefits for With Profit and Deposit Account type Plans usually assume the continuation of the *current* bonus or dividend rates. Some Plans show projected benefits with and without the inclusion of the terminal bonus. As pointed out previously, the terminal bonus is much more likely to fluctuate than the ordinary reversionary bonus so that projections including the terminal bonus should be treated with great caution.

The assumption that *current* reversionary bonus rates will remain unchanged over the next twenty to thirty years has come under some attack, particularly in the U.K. While bonus rates have not been cut since the second world war, and indeed have been increasing steadily, some experts now feel that with declining interest rates and an anticipated lower long-term rate of inflation, some Life Assurance Companies will find it difficult to maintain their current reversionary bonus rates in the future.

However, the concept of the reversionary bonus is that once declared it is a permanent addition to your Plan. It is also implied that there is a reasonable expectation that the current rate will continue to be paid over the future. Life Assurance Companies traditionally build up a surplus of reserve funds in order that they can maintain a stable reversionary bonus rate.

Many of the traditional Life Assurance Companies who operated solely on a With Profit basis have now switched to offering Unit-Linked versions of their Plans as well. The current trend is for a continuing increase in the amount of Unit-Linked business being transacted at the expense of With Profit Plans. This could therefore mean that the surplus or reserve built up by the Life Assurance Companies will be available in the future for a smaller than anticipated number of With Profit Policyholders. This could also help to maintain the bonus rate at the present level.

The assumption that current bonus rates will be maintained is more reasonable over a shorter period then over a longer period. For example, someone aged 55 taking out a plan to mature at age 65 would have a higher degree of confidence that the bonus rate would be maintained than, for example, a man aged 36 next birthday effecting a similar Plan to mature on his 65th birthday.

A with-profit Personal Pension Policy from one Life Office maturing in early 1985 for a male age 65 gave the following accumulated fund for 10 annual contributions of £1,000:

Guaranteed Fund	£11,040
Reversionary Bonuses	9,492
Terminal Bonus	2,760
	£23,292

This return represents a return on the contributions paid of approximately 14.9% p.a. The average inflation rate over the same period was 13.5%.

The same comments regarding the assumed annuity rates and allowance for inflation would apply equally to the With Profit projections as they would to the Unit-Linked ones.

However, if future bonus rates do fall as some people feel they must in the future, then this may be accompanied by lower inflation so that the 'real' value of the resulting benefits may be higher. In other words, the actual accumulated fund at retirement may be less in *monetary terms* than the originally projected amount, but the real or purchasing value may be greater than originally envisaged.

2.17 HOW MUCH SHOULD YOU CONTRIBUTE TO A RETIREMENT ANNUITY?

It might seem to be stating the obvious to say that the benefits which you can expect to obtain from your Retirement Annuity will be in direct proportion to the amount you contribute.

Your objective in contributing should be to provide an income in retirement which will allow you to maintain your standard of living at the desired level. In this case, you will want an income which is related to your earnings close to retirement — for example, an income of ⅔rds or maybe ½ of your earnings at retirement.

To achieve this objective, you should therefore think in terms of contributing a proportion of your salary to a Retirement Annuity rather than a fixed monetary amount. In other words, you should think of, for example, contributing 10% of your earnings to a Plan rather than £2,000 per annum. If you do this, then the contribution to your Retirement Annuity Plan or Plans will increase in line with your earnings and also hopefully in line with inflation.

If you do contribute a certain percentage of your earnings each year to a Retirement Annuity Plan, then your benefits will depend on three factors:-

(1) Your earnings between now and retirement.

(2) The investment return which your Plan will give you.

(3) Interest rates and hence annuity rates at retirement.

To give an example of the type of contribution rates which might be required to provide certain benefits, let us make the following assumptions:-

(1) That your earnings will increase at the rate of 7% per annum between now and retirement.

(2) The investment return on your Retirement Annuity Plan, after allowing for expenses, will be 9% per annum between now and retirement.

(3) That annuity rates at retirement will correspond to the long-term interest rate of 10% per annum and that inflation after retirement will average 6% per annum.

If it was therefore desired to provide an income in retirement, of half of your earnings, increasing in line with the cost of living, then the contribution rate required, expressed as a percentage of your current earnings, for the projected benefits would be as follows:-

Age next	Contribution rate as % of earnings	Current earnings	Projected earnings at 65	Projected pension at 65	Pension as % of earnings at 65
		£	£	£	%
35	12.6%	25,000	203,628	101,606	50
40	15.8%	25,000	145,183	72,564	50
45	20.6%	25,000	103,514	51,824	50
50	28.4%	25,000	73,804	36,848	50
55	43.4%	25,000	52,621	26,319	50

It should be remembered that the contribution rates set out above to provide the projected benefits are based on certain assumptions which may or may not be borne out.

Although the maximum limit for income tax relief purposes is set at 15%, there is in fact no reason why you cannot contribute more than this rate.

Ultimately, the rate at which you contribute to your Plan will depend on your financial circumstances from time to time and on the projected level of income which you feel you may require in retirement. The main point though is that if you wish to provide an income related to your earnings at retirement, then you should set your contribution as a percentage of earnings rather than a monetary amount.

2.18 WHICH RETIREMENT ANNUITY PLAN SHOULD YOU CHOOSE?

After deciding how much and at what rate you should contribute, the second most important point is obviously which Plan you invest your money in. There are a wide range of Plans available in the market and the choice can seem confusing.

Ultimately, choosing a particular Retirement Annuity Plan or Plans is really an investment decision — which Life Assurance Company is likely to give the highest investment return related to the degree of risk which you are willing to accept. Risk and return can never be divorced in investment decisions.

The degree of risk which is acceptable will vary from individual to individual, depending on personal circumstances.

Some of the factors which might be taken into account in determining an acceptable level of risk for investing in a Retirement Annuity would include:

(1) *Other Sources of Income:*
Do you expect to have any other source of income in retirement apart from the Retirement Annuity? For example, any Pensions from previous employment or Social Welfare Pensions. Are you likely to be in receipt of investment income? Are you likely to inherit property between now and retirement age?

(2) *Your Business:*
Many self-employed people look on their business as their Pension for retirement. Do you intend to sell your business at retirement or pass it on to your children? Is the value of your business likely to increase between now and retirement date or is its value likely to fluctuate widely?

(3) *Flexible Retirement Age:*
Is your business of such a nature that you must retire at a particular age or will you have great flexibility in deciding the timing or your retirement? Can you continue your occupation indefinitely?

(4) *Other Savings:*
Have you other savings put aside for your retirement, other than the Retirement Annuity? Do you intend to invest other funds in other outlets other than your Retirement Annuity?

The answer may well be, depending on the rate at which you wish to contribute to your Retirement Annuity, a portfolio approach. In other words, the question is not whether you invest all of your funds in one Retirement Annuity as opposed to another, but maybe possibly spreading it among different types of Plan and different Companies.

The same type of Plan cannot be suitable for everyone. For example, Unit-Linked type Plans are more suitable where you can accept a higher degree of risk and where you anticipate having considerable flexibility regarding the time at which you take your benefits. On the other hand, With Profit Plans might be more suitable for people much closer to retirement age who anticipate their main source of income in retirement coming from their Retirement Annuity.

3. LIFE ASSURANCE

3.1 LIFE ASSURANCE

When considering providing security for retirement, you should also consider the question of providing security for your dependants in the event of your death before retirement age. One natural way of providing this type of security is through the medium of Life Assurance.

Government statistics show that approximately one out of four men now aged 40 will die before reaching age 65. The odds are very similar at other ages. It is therefore a risk that should be considered and provided for.

3.2 DEATH BENEFIT UNDER RETIREMENT ANNUITIES

As pointed out in the previous chapter, most Retirement Annuity Plans provide a lump sum death benefit in the event of death before retirement age. Under most Plans, it is invariably a return of contributions paid to the date of death, with interest. Therefore, in the earlier years the sum payable on death is unlikely to be very large. For example, this table below sets out the estimated refund on death in the case of a Unit-Linked Plan assuming a unit growth rate of 13% per annum:

Number of years contributions paid	Amount payable on death per £1,000 annual contribution
	£
5	6,408
10	17,841
15	38,787
20	77,459
25	150,018

The above figures assume a person aged 40 next birthday at entry. Therefore, in the earlier years of a Plan, the amount of life cover would not be very large. Additional life assurance protection may well be required, depending on the amount of any existing cover which you might have.

3.3 SECTION 235(A) LIFE ASSURANCE

There is a form of Life Assurance available only to people who are eligible to take out a Retirement Annuity. This Life Assurance is often referred to as Section 235A after the section in the Income Tax Act 1967, which provides for this type of Life Assurance cover. Therefore, if you are eligible to take out a Retirement Annuity, you are eligible to effect this Life Assurance cover as well.

Section 235A Life Assurance cover is the same as any other form of Life Assurance in that it provides a lump sum on death in return for a certain level of premium.

There are various forms of life cover — life cover for a ten year period, or life cover to the chosen retirement age such as 60, 65 or 70.

The main advantage of Section 235A Life Assurance is that the full premium can be offset for income tax purposes as opposed to only half of the premium in the case of ordinary Life Assurance. The full premium is tax deductable up to a limit of 5% of net relevant earnings. This 5% limit is inclusive of the overall limit of 15% of net relevant earnings for Retirement Annuity purposes. In other words, if you are claiming tax relief for this type of Life Assurance cover up to the limit of 5% of net relevant earnings, then your limit for Retirement Annuity purposes is 10%.

Because of differing taxation rules applying to Life Assurance Companies, the premiums for Section 235A Life Assurance are generally *dearer* than a similar type of cover under ordinary Life Assurance. On the other hand, you can write the full premium off, up to the 5% limit, for tax purposes as opposed to half with normal Life Assurance.

3.4 ORDINARY LIFE ASSURANCE

As pointed out in the previous paragraph, you could always effect ordinary Life Assurance cover. You can claim income tax relief on half of the premium at your top rate of tax, subject to an overall limit of £1,000 premiums for single person and £2,000 per annum for a married couple.

3.5 SECTION 235A OR ORDINARY LIFE ASSURANCE?

If you do decide to effect Life Assurance cover, then should you do it under Section 235A or go for an ordinary Life Assurance Policy?

There is an income tax relief advantage in going for the Section 235A as opposed to ordinary Life Assurance. However, this eats into the 15% overall limit for Retirement Annuity purposes so that you may be able to claim less income tax relief in respect of your Retirement Annuity than might otherwise have been the case.

Generally speaking, ordinary Life Assurance Policies are probably a better bet for the following reasons:-

(1) There is a more attractive and flexible range of Contracts available for ordinary Life Assurance than are currently available for Section 235A. These ordinary Policies are generally more flexible with regard to increasing cover in line with inflation and other conditions.

(2) Under the Section 235A Policy, the lump sum death benefit must be paid to your personal representatives and hence into your Estate on death. However, with an ordinary Life Assurance Policy, it may be possible to arrange it on a ''Life of Another'' basis or arrange the Policy under trust for the benefit of your dependants. In this case, the proceeds could be paid direct on death to your next of kin without the delay associated with obtaining Grant of Probate etc.

(3) However, the most serious disadvantage of the Section 235A policies is that you must stop contributing to the policy and hence cover must cease if you cease to be eligible by, for example, ceasing to be self-employed and joining a Company Pension Scheme. Also cover must cease under a Section 235A policy at age 70 at the latest.

3.6 COST

The cost of Life Assurance depends on a number of factors: your age, sex, the amount of cover, the length of time the cover is required, whether you smoke or not, and your general state of health at the time you take out the Policy.

Assuming that you are in good health and are acceptable for life assurance at first class terms, the following table shows the annual premiums of £50,000 cover to age 60, and 65.

£50,000 Sum Assured

Age next/now	To age 60 Section 235A £	Ordinary £	To age 65 Section 235A £	Ordinary £
35	207.00	204.95	241.35	261.40
40	272.55	261.80	321.70	334.25
45	367.50	339.65	436.55	432.70
50	504.05	443.30	595.60	562.40

Notes:

(1) The above rates apply to male smokers. Females and non-smokers would benefit from cheaper rates.

(2) In the case of the Section 235A policy, cover would cease on the 60th or 65th birthday as appropriate. For the ordinary Life Assurance Policy, the cover ceases on the Policy anniversary preceding the 60th or 65th birthday as appropraite.

Generally speaking, the sooner you start, the cheaper the premium is.

4. DISABILITY INSURANCE

4.1 DISABILITY INSURANCE

A particular risk facing the self-employed is the loss of income in the event of long term sickness or disability. By definition self-employed people often work on their own and are dependant for their income on their own efforts. As will be seen in the Social Insurance Section the self-employed are not covered for sickness and disability benefit under the Social Welfare Schemes.

However, if you are self-employed, then you can consider effecting a Disability Insurance or Permanent Health Insurance policy. This Policy would provide you with a certain level of income in the event of a loss of income due to you being unable to work because of sickness or disability.

4.2 DEFINITION OF DISABILITY

It is important to appreciate when a benefit is payable under a Disability Insurance Policy. It is not sufficient merely to be sick or disabled. You must be sick and disabled *and* unable to carry on working. The essential feature of Disability Insurance is the provision of an income only where there is a *loss of income* due to sickness or disability. The usual definition is that there must be a loss of earnings due to sickness or disability and "you are unable to carry on your normal occupation or any other occupation for which you are suitably qualified". In some cases a partial benefit may be payable where you are able to return to your work on a part time basis and hence there is only a part loss of earnings.

4.3 DEFERRED PERIOD

Benefit is usually payable after a certain period of continuous sickness referred to as the "deferred period". The common deferred periods are 13 weeks, 26 weeks and 52 weeks. The longer the deferred period chosen, the cheaper the cost of the insurance. You should obviously choose a longer deferred period if your occupation is one where your earnings will continue for a certain period, even if you cease working on a full-time basis. On the other hand, if your earnings are likely to cease immediately should you become sick or disabled, then you should go for the shorter deferred period such as 13 weeks.

4.3 WAIVER OF PREMIUM

It is common in Disability Insurance Policies for the premium itself to be waived in the event of a claim. Therefore, should benefit be payable to you, you would receive the regular income and would not be required to pay any further premiums until benefit ceases.

4.4 PAYMENT OF BENEFIT

Payment of benefit commences after the deferred period and continues until you return to work or reach the chosen termination age, which is usually your 60th or 65th birthday at which the Policy ceases.

4.5 INCREASES IN BENEFITS

Most Disability Insurance Policies contain an option, for an extra premium, whereby the benefit in the course of payment can be increased at a certain rate — for example 5% or 7.5% per annum. Most Plans also now contain an option, again in return for an extra premium, whereby the amount of cover can be increased by a certain amount at regular intervals, without fresh evidence of health. A few Plans will increase the cover in line with inflation on a regular basis.

4.6 BENEFIT RESTRICTIONS

Most Disability Insurance Plans operated by Insurance Companies contain a restriction whereby the benefit, regardless of the actual amount of cover being paid for, will be restricted to a certain amount such as 75% of earnings less any social welfare disability benefits. The basic reason for this is that it is felt that there should always be a financial incentive to return to work rather than continuing to claim Disability Insurance benefit.

4.7 COST

Disability Insurance premiums are charged in relation to the amount of income insured. The cost will depend on the age at the commencement of the Plan, your sex, the deferred period chosen, the termination age chosen and your state of health then.

For example, a benefit of £10,000 per annum for a male aged 45 next birthday, with a deferred period of 26 weeks and terminating at the 65th birthday, would cost approximately £283 per annum from one Company. Additional premiums would be payable if increases in the amount of cover and increases in benefit payment were required.

There are often loadings added to the premiums depending on occupation. If your occupation is of such a nature that the Insurance Company feels you run an increased risk of becoming sick or disabled, then an extra premium or loading may be imposed. In extreme cases, the Insurance Company may refuse to accept the risk at all and refuse to cover you.

4.8 EXCLUSIONS

If you have had a medical history of a serious nature, it may still be possible to obtain Disability Insurance but there may well be "exclusions" on the cover. An exclusion is an endorsement on the Policy so as to exclude payment of benefit in connection with periods of sickness or disablement which are directly attributable to your particular medical impairment. For example, if you had had a history of high blood pressure, then your Policy might exclude payment of benefit in respect of sickness connected with this problem. These restrictions would include self-inflicted injuries and sickness as a result of alcoholism.

4.9 TAXATION

Since 1979, it is possible to claim income tax relief on Disability Insurance premiums. An individual may claim income tax relief in any year in respect of approved Disability Insurance Policies on premiums to 10% of income. The full premium is deductible against your marginal rate of tax up to the 10% limit.

If you claim income tax relief on the premiums then if benefit becomes payable, it is taxable immediately. In fact, the Insurance Company will operate the P.A.Y.E. system on the payment of benefit.

On the other hand, if you do not claim income tax relief on the premium, then the benefit is not taxable until it is received by you for one complete tax year. You would therefore get at least one tax year with the benefit free of tax.

In most cases, people prefer to claim income tax relief at the expense of having the benefit taxable immediately in the event of a claim.

4.10 CHOICE OF COMPANY

Choosing a Disability Insurance policy should not be based solely on a comparison of costs. For example, if Company A was charging £300 p.a., while Company B was charging £200 p.a., for the same cover in each case, it should not be taken blindly that Company B is offering the better value for money. With Disability Insurance, the terms and conditions of the policy document are vital. The vital question is in what circumstances will benefit be payable and in what circumstances will benefit *not* be payable. In the above example, Company B was quoting a cheaper premium but it may not have been providing as comprehensive coverage as the plan from Company A.

II Pensions for the Employee

In this section we are dealing with the various Pension options open to employees in both the public and private sectors. Private sector employees are covered in Chapters 5 and 6 while public sector and civil servants are covered in Chapter 7.

You do not have to work for a Company to be an employee. You could be employed by another individual or by a Partnership — such as a firm of Accountants or Solicitors.

By "employee" in this section we are referring to people who are liable to income tax in respect of their earnings under Schedule E.

5. EMPLOYEES

5.1 INTRODUCTION

In this chapter, we are dealing with occupational Pension Schemes for employees in the private sector.

Of course, many employers may not have a Company Pension Scheme for their employees. There is no compulsion on an employer to provide one for his employees. In this chapter we outline the *maximum* benefits which can be provided under a Pension Scheme by an employer for an employee. If you are in a Company Pension Scheme, your benefits may well be less than the maximum outlined here.

A Pension Scheme established by an employer for his employees usually provides two separate benefits:

(1) Retirement benefits.

(2) Death Benefits.

A Pension Scheme does not have to provide any minimum level of benefits — the restriction is only on the maximum level which can be provided.

5.2 REVENUE COMMISSIONERS

The legislation covering employee Pension Schemes is set out in the 1972 Finance Act. However, this legislation merely sets down the broad guidelines and the day to day regulation of these Schemes is left up to the Revenue Commissioners — Retirement Benefits Division.

To qualify for the maximum tax advantages, which will be discussed later, a Pension Scheme must qualify as an "exempt approved" Scheme. An exempt approved scheme is a Pension Scheme which is approved by the Revenue Commissioners as providing benefits within the maximum level and which is established under "irrevocable trust".

This leads to the important point that a Pension Scheme has a separate legal existance from that of the employer and the employees. Setting the Scheme up under "irrevocable trust" means that any contributions paid into the Scheme are legally no longer in the ownership of either the employer or the employees. A Trust is usually created into which are paid all the contributions and from which are drawn the various benefits being provided.

A Pension Scheme therefore has four parties:

(1) The Employer — who agrees initially to set up the Scheme and who undertakes the main financial burden of providing the benefits.

(2) The Scheme Members — who are the employees covered by the Scheme.

(3) The Trustee — who is the individual or individuals or Company who have the responsibility and duty of collecting the contributions, investing them and paying benefits.

(4) The Administrator — who is the person or persons having the management of the Scheme. The Administrator, in some cases, can be liable to tax on the happening of certain events in a Pension Scheme, such as the tax due on the refund of a member's contributions on leaving service.

To qualify for all the tax advantages, a Pension Scheme must first of all be approved by the Revenue Commissioners. If a Scheme is approved, then it must not provide benefits in excess of the maximum benefits which are currently allowed by the Revenue Commissioners.

In the following sections, we are outlining the *maximum* benefits which can be provided in certain eventualities. Very few Schemes indeed would provide all of these maximum benefits in all areas.

5.3 RETIREMENT BENEFITS

The main purpose of a Pension Scheme is to provide a Pension in retirement for its members.

The normal practice is to express the Pension as being a fraction of your final remuneration for each year of service with your employer up to retirement age. For example, a common scale is to provide a Pension of 1/60th of your final remuneration at retirement for each year of service up to a maximum of ⅔rds.

The maximum Pension which can be provided at your retirement age is in accordance with the following table:

Years of Service to retirement age with employer	Maximum pension as a fraction of final remuneration
1 - 5	1/60th for each year.
6	8/60ths
7	16/60ths
8	24/60ths
9	32/60ths
10	40/60ths

The above maximum Pension fractions are inclusive of any other retained benefits which you might have from previous Pension Schemes, with previous employers.

The Revenue allow this maximum pension to be increased in line with the cost of living during retirement. However, very few private sector companies promise to increase pensions in this way. A more usual promised increase would be 5% p.a. Many employers tend to increase pensions in payment on an *ad-hoc* basis, from year to year.

Pensions are liable to income tax and the payer of the pension usually operates PAYE in payment.

Normal retirement age is usually in the range 60 to 70 for males and 55 to 70 for females.

"Final remuneration" will usually be defined as one of the following:

(1) Your remuneration for any one of the five years preceding retirement age or

(2) Your average remuneration for any three or more consecutive years ending not earlier than ten years before retirement age or

(3) Your remuneration at the date of retirement or at any date within the year preceding retirement.

"Remuneration" means basic pay plus the average over a suitable period — usually three or more years — of any fluctuating payment such as commission or bonuses. However, while this is the maximum allowed by the Revenue, in practice many Schemes would exclude fluctuating payments such as commission or bonuses in their definition of remuneration and hence of final remuneration for pension purposes.

Benefits in kind may also be taken into account where they are assessed under Schedule E for the purposes of defining remuneration. Again, however, it is common to find that BIKs are not included in the definition of remuneration for pension purposes.

However, it may be possible for you to pension your own benefit-in-kinds under a top-up arrangement. This is discussed in more detail in Chapter 8, under the heading of "Topping-Up your Pension".

5.4 CASH LUMP SUM

It is normally possible to commute part or all of your Pension for a tax-free cash lump sum at retirement age. In some cases, the cash lump sum may be provided *in addition* to your Pension benefit. Indeed, it is possible to set up a Pension Scheme to provide a cash gratuity only. The cash lump sum benefit is usually expressed as a fraction of your final remuneration at retirement age for each year of service up to that date. The common fraction allowed by the Revenue is 3/80ths for each year with a maximum cash sum of 1½ times your final remuneration. The maximum scale is as follows:-

The total value of the Pension and cash lump sum may not exceed ⅔rds of your final remuneration. For the purposes of converting Pension to lump sum and vice versa most Pension Schemes would have an agreed set of "commutation" factors for this purpose,

Years of service to retirement age	Maximum lump sum as a fraction of final remuneration
1 - 8	3/80ths for each year
9	30/80ths
10	36/80ths
11	42/80ths
12	48/80ths
13	54/80ths
14	63/80ths
15	72/80ths
16	81/80ths
17	90/80ths
18	99/80ths
19	108/80ths
20 or more	120/80ths

that is a factor to convert pension to cash and vice versa. For example, it might be set out that regardless of retirement age or sex, each £1 pension is worth £9 of cash. Alternatively, a scale varying by retirement age and sex might be used.

5.5 EARLY RETIREMENT

You may normally retire early at any stage on grounds of serious ill-health. In this case, the *maximum* benefit allowed is an immediate pension equal to the maximum pension which you could have received had you remained in service until your normal retirement age but based on your remuneration at the date of early retirement.

If, for example, you had joined the Pension Scheme at age 30, and your normal retirement age was 65, then your total prospective service would be 35 years. If you retired at age 40 on grounds of serious ill-health, then the Pension Scheme might give you a pension based on 35/60ths of your final remuneration at the date of early retirement. You can effectively get credit for years of service which you would have expected to complete up to retirement age.

If your Pension Scheme allows, you may normally retire early on grounds other than ill-health at any time after your 50th birthday. However, in this case the maximum pension which can be provided immediately would be the maximum approvable pension at retirement age, but based on your present remuneration, reduced to allow for the shorter completed service to the date of your actual early retirement.

For example, if you had joined the Pension Scheme at age 30, with a normal retirement age of 65, then your total prospective service is 35 years. If your Pension Scheme promised you 1/60th of your final remuneration for each year of service, then your prospective pension is obviously 35/60ths of your final remuneration. If you retire early at age 50, then your actual completed service to that date would be 20 years. In this case, the maximum pension which can be provided at age 50 is 20/35 x 40/60 x final remuneration at age 50. Again, part of this Pension may be commuted for a cash lump sum based on the service completed to the date of retirement. Although the Revenue will allow this pension to be paid in full, it is usual for many Schemes to reduce this pension by a factor such as ½% for each month to age 65 from the date of early retirement. This reduction normally does not apply in the case of ill-health early retirement.

5.6 EMPLOYEES CONTRIBUTIONS

Some Schemes are non-contributory whereas others make it mandatory for employees who join the Scheme to contribute at a certain level — for example 5% of earnings. Where fluctuating earnings such as commission and bonuses are not pensioned, then it is usual that your contributions do not apply to these earnings.

You can contribute and claim full income tax relief on contributions of up to 15% of your earnings in any one tax year. Relief is allowed in full at your marginal rate of tax.

Your contribution is usually deducted from your pay at source by your employer so that you receive immediate relief from income tax and indeed P.R.S.I. When your contribution is deducted at source in this manner, you pay income tax and P.R.S.I. on your income *after* the deduction of the Pension contribution.

5.7 EMPLOYERS CONTRIBUTIONS

Unlike the employee, the employer must contribute to the Pension Plan. The Revenue require that in the normal case, the employer will, by normal retirement age, have contributed not less than 1/3rd of the cost of the benefits for each employee.

Employer's contributions to a Pension Scheme are also fully

allowable as a trading expense for tax purposes. In cases where an employer would make a special lump sum contribution, possibly to top up the Pension Scheme, then tax relief may be spread over a number of years. Where a Scheme is an exempt approved Scheme, any contribution which your employer makes to the Scheme on your behalf is *not* treated as a benefit in kind.

5.8 DEATH-IN-SERVICE BENEFITS

A Pension Scheme may also provide benefits for your next of kin in the event of your death prior to retirement age.

The maximum lump sum which may be paid is four times your final remuneration at the date of death together with a refund of any contributions, with or without interest, which you may have paid prior to your death. Usually the lump sum is paid to your Estate but it may be paid to a nominated beneficiary or distributed at the discretion of the Trustees of the Pension Scheme.

In addition, a Pension may be provided for your spouse and other dependants. The maximum pension which can be provided for your spouse, or where there is no spouse, for a dependant, is 2/3rds of the maximum pension that could have been provided for you if you had retired on grounds of ill-health at the date of your death.

As your own maximum Pension, assuming that you would have completed at least ten years service to retirement age, would be 2/3rds of your final remuneration, the maximum spouses pension then effectively becomes 4/9ths of your final remuneration at the date of death. Additional pensions may be provided for other dependants such as children but no one pension may exceed the maximum for the spouse and the total of all pensions must not exceed the maximum prospective pension which you could have received yourself on retirement — for example 2/3rds of your final remuneration.

It is often common to find that widows pensions are specified as ceasing on death or earlier remarriage. Childrens pensions often continue up to age 18 or age 21 if the child is in receipt of full-time education.

5.9 DEATH-IN-RETIREMENT BENEFITS

A Pension Scheme may also provide for spouses and dependants pensions to become payable in the event of your death after you have started to draw your own pension.

The maximum spouses pension which may be provided is 2/3rds of the maximum pension which you could have received at retirement age. As for death-in-service benefits, dependants pensions may also be provided so that the total of the spouses and dependants pensions does not exceed the full amount of the maximum pension which could have been provided for yourself at retirement.

Again, the widows pension may continue for life or it may cease on remarriage. Similarly, the childrens pension must cease at age 18 or 21 if the child is in full-time education.

Alternatively, or indeed in addition to any specific spouses and dependants pensions, you can normally choose to surrender part of your own pension to provide a pension for your widow or widower or dependants which would commence on your death. The main restriction is that the total of these dependants and widows pensions should not exceed the remaining pension for yourself. The terms for surrendering part of your pension in exchange for a widows pension may be set out in the Scheme or may be the subject of a calculation by an actuary appointed to the Fund.

5.10 LEAVING YOUR EMPLOYMENT

If you leave the service of your employer and hence the Pension Scheme, for any reason other than by death or retirement, then the three main options available to you are as follows:-

(1) A refund of your own contributions, with or without interest, where you were contributing to the Scheme.

(2) A deferred or frozen pension and/or a deferred lump sum payable at your normal retirement age.

(3) The payment of a transfer value to a new Pension Scheme which you might be joining.

If your Pension Scheme is contributory and you take a refund of your contributions on leaving service, then you are not entitled to receive any other benefit from the Scheme.

Where you take a refund of your contributions you will normally be liable to tax on 10% of the refund. You will therefore receive 90% of your contributions paid. If the Scheme is contributory and you decide to leave your contributions within the Scheme, then you may also be entitled to benefit from some part of the employers contributions paid on your behalf up to the date of leaving.

A deferred or frozen Pension is usually calculated by reference to remuneration, in whatever way it is defined for the purpose of the Pension Scheme, at the date of leaving service and taking into account actual service completed to the date of withdrawal. While the Revenue Commissioners will allow this deferred or frozen Pension to be increased in line with inflation up to the date of your actual retirement, the vast majority of Schemes do not in fact provide for this indexation. Hence these deferred pensions are often called "frozen" pensions.

For example, let us assume that your current Pension Plan provides you with a Pension of 1/60th of your final remuneration at age 65, subject to a maximum Pension of 2/3rds. You joined the Scheme ten years ago at age 25 and you are now leaving service at a current salary of £15,000 per annum. If the Pension Scheme rules allow, you may be entitled to a Pension of 10/60ths of £15,000 — that is £2,500 per annum in thirty years time at age 65.

However, almost certainly your Pension Scheme will not provide for any increases to be made in this figure between now and the date of payment in thirty years time, when its purchasing value will obviously be much reduced.

Where your Pension Scheme is non-contributory, or where you have been contributing but on leaving you decided to leave your contributions within the Pension Fund, your right to a deferred or frozen Pension in respect of your employer's contributions may not necessarily be automatic.

The entitlement to benefits under a Scheme on leaving service is often referred to as "vested rights". Such rights are not automatic in many Pension Schemes and in others are only available after a certain minimum period of service such as five years. Therefore, in a case where you are not entitled to vested rights on leaving service, you would have no entitlement to a deferred pension or only a small one in respect of your own contributions, where you decided to leave these contributions within the Fund. With job mobility now becoming more common, it is very important to check the details of your Pension Scheme to see what benefits, if any, you would be entitled to on leaving service. This point is considered in more detail in paragraph 5.15, "Portable Pensions".

5.11 SOCIAL WELFARE PENSIONS

Membership of a Pension Scheme does not affect your entitlement to any Pension under the Social Insurance Schemes. If you are paying the appropriate contribution rate — for example Class Al — and have sufficient contributions at retirement, you will be entitled to the Retirement or Old Age Pension regardless of any other Pension you may become entitled to from your employment.

However, your Pension entitlement under the Pension Scheme may take account of part of your Social Insurance Pension benefits. For example, it is common in many Schemes to find that the maximum Pension is defined as 2/3rds of final salary less the contributory Old Age Pension at the single persons rate. Based on the present Pension rate of £51.40 weekly, this means that the Pension Scheme might provide a maximum pension of 2/3rds of final remuneration less £2,673 per annum.

For example, if your final remuneration was £20,000 per annum, then your Pension Scheme might provide you with a Pension of 2/3rds x £20,000 - £2,673 = £10,660 per annum.

The basic idea is that your Pension from the Pension Scheme when added to the single persons Contributory Old Age Pension will in total give an amount equal to 2/3rds of your final remuneration. The inclusion of Social Welfare benefits in this manner is often referred to as "integration with Social Welfare".

For Schemes integrated in such a way, it is often common to find that all Pension Scheme benefits are based on "pensionable salary". Pensionable salary in turn is defined as your basic salary less a deduction equal to 1½ times the current non-contributory Old Age (single persons rate) benefit. For example, based on the present benefit of £51.40 weekly, the deduction to arrive at pensionable salary would be £4,009. Your pension benefits might therefore be expressed as l/60th of your final pensionable salary for each year of service up to a maximum of 2/3rds of final pensionable salary. Obviously your "pensionable salary" will vary from year to year in line with your own increasing salary and the increasing level of Social Welfare benefits.

5.12 FUNDING

A Pension Scheme is a promise by your employer to provide you and your dependants with certain benefits on death or retirement. Your employer must obviously put funds aside now to meet these future obligations. In some cases, you may also be contributing.

Pension Schemes in Ireland and the U.K. operate on the basis of building up a fund to meet these obligations. In some countries, such as France, many Schemes operate on the "pay as you go basis" — in other words, the employer pays for the benefits each year as they occur.

The concept of building up a fund is important for two reasons:-

(1) *Security:*
The Pension Fund assets are held outside of the employers direct control and are not subject to the fluctuating fortunes of his business.

(2) *Investment Return:*
By putting funds aside on a regular basis in advance, these funds can be invested and the investment return added to the accumulating fund.

The basic operation of a Pension Fund over time can be stated by this simplified formula:

$C + I = B + E$ where
C = Employers and Employees contributions paid into fund.
I = Investment Return on pension assets.
B = Benefits paid out to Members.
E = Expenses of managing the Fund.

It is obvious from the above simple formula that unless the contribution income and investment return of the fund are sufficient then the promised benefits cannot ultimately be paid. Therefore, while your employer and the Pension Scheme may promise you certain pension benefits at retirement, these benefits cannot be paid unless the Pension Fund has been maintained at a sufficient level.

Most of the larger Pension Funds have an Actuary appointed to the Fund who is responsible for the regular valuation of the Fund and recommending a contribution rate sufficient to meet the benefits being promised, after taking account of existing Pension Fund assets. However, the Actuary cannot force the employer to make the required contribution rate. If the employer is experiencing difficult trading conditions then he may well decide to cut back on his contribution.

In recent years, this whole topic has come to the forefront as many Companies have gone into liquidation and made employees redundant. In many cases, the employees were shocked to find that the Pension Fund was in deficit. In other words, there simply was not sufficient assets available to provide the various benefits promised.

This problem can arise due to a combination of many factors. However, the basic problem is that many Schemes are not "funded" up to an appropriate level. The degree of funding in a Scheme at any point is often calculated by comparing the value of the Scheme assets compared with the estimated value of the Scheme liabilities, assuming the Scheme is terminated at that stage. For example, if you had completed half of your potential service, you would expect half of your potential pension at retirement age, allowing for future salary increases to be secured, but only a small minority of Schemes are able to satisfy these criteria. Most Schemes would, in this example, have sufficient assets to provide a pension at retirement age based on your *current* salary but not on the salary that you could have expected to retire on. However, a considerable amount of Schemes would not even satisfy this diluted standard of funding, either because the Scheme was introduced recently and promises benefits for prior service, which are being paid for by future contributions, or because benefits have recently been improved, or simply because the Company is not contributing enough to the Fund.

The degree of funding, and hence the security of your benefits is not easy to determine — particularly if you are not a pension expert.

5.13 PENSION FUND INVESTMENTS

Employers and employees contributions to the Pension Fund are invested to build up the fund. Pension Funds usually invest their assets in one of two ways:

(1) *Self-Administered:*
For the larger Funds the investment is often conducted on what is called a "self-administered" basis. In other words, the Pension Fund Trustees would, in conjunction with some professional Investment Manager, buy Government Gilts, Equities, Properties etc., and hold these assets direct. Some

of the larger funds might split the investment management of the fund between a few different Investment Managers.

(2) *"Insured" Approach:*
Under this method, the Trustees would invest their monies with a Life Assurance Company in such a manner so as to obtain some minimum guaranteed return. This method would in many ways be akin to a With Profit Retirement Annuity as discussed in Chapter 2.

The term "Insured" arose from the fact that the Trustees were "insuring" part of their investment risk by obtaining some form of guaranteed return from the Life Assurance Company. However the guarantee, if any, would be a monetary one and not a "real" one in the sense of guaranteeing a return in line with inflation.

The distinction between the self-administered and insured approach has blurred considerably in recent years. Most Life Assurance Companies now run Pension Unit funds for the larger Pension Funds where they can purchase units. There would be no minimum return guaranteed in respect of these units so that for all intents and purposes, the investment is akin to the self-administered route.

Many smaller Pension Schemes catering for one or more individual employees often operate on the basis of a separate investment type of Policy taken out with a Life Assurance Company in respect of each employee covered in the Scheme. In many cases these Policies are linked to Unit Funds operated by the Life Assurance Companies and so carry no minimum guaranteed return. In other cases, the Policies may be of a with profit type where there would be some guarantees.

Most Pension Funds, be they large or small, insure their Death Benefits with a Life Assurance Company. Therefore, on the death of a Pension Scheme Member, the Life Assurance Company pay the appropriate sum to the Pension Fund Trustees who in turn pay it in lump sum and/or Pension form, as appropriate, to the next of kin.

5.14 "MONEY PURCHASE" SCHEMES

So far in this chapter we have been considering what are often called "Defined Benefit" Schemes. In other words, Pension

Schemes whereby benefits are defined in some manner or other — usually related to your salary. For example, a Pension Scheme which promises you a maximum pension of 2/3rds of your final remuneration would be a Defined Benefits Scheme.

However, in recent years there has been a trend away from the Defined Benefit type Scheme to the Money Purchase or Defined Contributions type arrangement, particularly for the smaller Pension Fund.

The concept behind Money Purchase arrangements is that the benefits provided by the Scheme will be those which can be provided by the contributions made to the Scheme. For example, if your employer decided to set up a one-man Pension Arrangement for yourself, he might decide to commit himself to contributing 10% of your salary each year to the Plan. Your benefits under the Plan, therefore, would be the benefits which can ultimately be paid out of the fund accumulated to the date of retirement. However, there is an over-riding maximum level of benefit as outlined in previous paragraphs which the Revenue Commissioners stipulate must apply to all approved Pension Schemes. The maximum pension, for example, is 2/3rds of your final remuneration at the date of retirement.

Money Purchase Schemes usually operate on the basis of an individual policy being effected with a Life Assurance Company in respect of each employee covered.

These Schemes are more popular with employers for small groups of employees as they allow the employer to budget more closely for his Pension Scheme outlay. In the case of a Scheme promising a defined level of benefit, regular valuations are required by the Actuary and there may be adjustments to the contribution rate if, for example, salaries have been increasing at a faster rate than allowed for or investments have not earned as much as anticipated. Many employers like the fact that under Money Purchase Arrangement, their costs are controlled and are not open-ended. The employer can stop, start, increase or decrease the level of contribution as circumstances change.

From the employee's point of view, the money purchase route can offer greater security in that the employee knows how much the employer is setting aside for his pension. The defined benefit scheme, on the other hand, can give a false sense of security in that it promises certain retirement benefits but the Pension Fund may not be able to support the promises if it has not been maintained at an adequate level.

5.15 PORTABLE PENSIONS

In recent years a debate has grown up in Ireland and the U.K. over "Portable Pensions".

The term "Portable Pensions" usually is taken to mean the right to carry your Pension rights with you from job to job up to retirement age.

This demand has arisen due to the fact that if you change jobs a number of times during your working lifetime you may well receive much lower benefits at retirement than you would have if you had remained with one employer throughout.

This is so because of the following:-

(1) If your previous Pension Scheme had been contributory then on leaving service you may well have been entitled to a refund of your contributions. As pointed out previously, if you accept this refund of contribution then you are not entitled to any deferred or frozen Pension from that Pension Scheme.

(2) Even in a non-contributory Scheme if you leave service you may or may not be entitled to a deferred or frozen pension from your employer depending on whether the Scheme has vested rights or not. As pointed out previously, even where Schemes do carry vested rights, it is often common to find that a certain minimum period of service is required in order to qualify for these. For example, five years is not an uncommon qualifying period.

(3) More importantly, even in a case where you have a right to a deferred or frozen Pension on leaving service, it will almost certainly be based on your salary at the time of leaving service and will not be increased in line with inflation up to the date of your retirement.

Although the Revenue Commissioners will allow this deferred or frozen Pension to be increased in line with inflation, the majority of Schemes do not do so due to the extra cost which this would impose on employers.

An example can show how this problem arises.

Let us say that you joined Company A at age 25 and were

included in their Pension Scheme for a Pension of 1/60th of final remuneration for each year of service to age 65 — in other words a maximum of 2/3rds of final remuneration. Let us say that you leave Company A at age 45 and join Company B with whom you remain until age 65.

Let us assume that your salary at the time of leaving Company A was £10,000 per annum and that you transferred to Company B at the same salary and it increased at the rate of 10% per annum over the next twenty years to retirement at age 65 to a final salary of £67,275 p.a.

Even if the Pension Scheme in Company A gave you a deferred or frozen Pension your Pensions at age 65 might work out as follows:-

Company A: 20/60ths x £10,000	=	£3,334 per annum.
Company B: 20/60ths x £67,275	=	£22,425 per annum.
Total Pension payable at 65	=	£25,759 per annum.

If you had joined Company B at age 25 and remained there for forty years, your final Pension would have been 2/3rds of final salary at age 65 — which would work out at a pension of 2/3 x £67,275 = £44,850 p.a. or 74% more than if you had changed jobs once at age 45.

The basic problem is that the deferred Pension from Company A is frozen at its level at the time of leaving, while on joining the new Scheme you may only obtain credit for service actually completed with them. You are therefore effectively penalised for changing jobs.

You may, in some cases, be able to bring your Pension with you where your previous Pension Scheme is willing to pay what is called a "transfer value" to your new Scheme. This transfer value represents a payment in lieu of maintaining the deferred pension for you. However, the problem is that your new Pension Scheme will not feel that this transfer value figure is enough to allow them to give you full credit for all your service with your previous employer.

The basic point at issue is whether a pension is a reward for service with an employer or a form of deferred compensation. If you look on it as a reward for long service with an employer then the present position whereby any deferred pension you might obtain on leaving employment is frozen, seems reasonable. If, however, you look on Pension rights as deferred compensation, then your deferred or frozen pension should be increased in line with the cost of living up to retirement age, to maintain its purchasing power.

5.16 NON-PENSIONABLE EMPLOYMENT

If you are in employment where there is presently no Pension Arrangement, then there are two options open to you:

(1) You could try to persuade your employer to set up and contribute to a Pension Arrangement for yourself. If he did, then you could also contribute up to 15% of your earnings and receive full tax relief. If it is a large company, the prospects of your employer agreeing to set up a special scheme for one person would seem remote.

(2) If (1) is not possible, then you can always contribute to a Retirement Annuity as explained in chapter 2. Your employer may not contribute to this, but you can contribute up to 15% of your earnings and receive full tax relief.

5.17 PENSION SCHEME BOOKLET

If you are a member of a Pension Scheme then you will almost certainly at some stage have been given a copy of the Pension Scheme booklet which sets out briefly the main benefits of the Scheme. If you have not got an up to date copy then you should certainly try to get one and study it closely.

Very few Schemes provide the maximum range of benefits as allowed by the Revenue. Some of the areas where your Scheme may fall short of the Revenue maximum are:

— Integration of benefits with Social Welfare Pensions.

— Definition of final remuneration which will usually exclude fluctuating items like commissions and Benefit-in-Kind liabilities.

— Increases in pensions in payment.

— Benefits on leaving service.

If your benefits are not up to the maximum allowed by the Revenue, then you can possibly top-up your pension at your own expense as explained in Chapter 8.

6. COMPANY DIRECTORS

6.1 CONTROLLING DIRECTORS

Up to 1974, controlling Directors could not be included in a Company Pension Scheme. A controlling director is deemed to be a director who is in a position, in conjunction with his family and any family trusts, to control more than 20% of the voting shares of the Company.

However, this restriction was lifted in 1974 and now controlling directors, who are working on a fulltime basis in the Company, may be included in a Company Pension Scheme in respect of any earnings assessible to income tax under Schedule E. However, there are some restrictions in respect of some of the benefits which may be provided for controlling Directors. These are explained later in this Chapter.

6.2 CONTRIBUTION RATES

While fulltime working Company Directors might look on themselves as being "self-employed" in fact for Pension Scheme purposes, they are treated as being an employee of the Company.

The maximum benefits which can be provided under a Pension Scheme for a Director are very generous indeed, as outlined in Chapter 5, so that the total amount which can be contributed by a Company and Director together to a Pension Plan, to provide these maximum benefits, are very high:

Age next at entry to pension scheme	Maximum annual retirement contribution (as % of salary)		
	Retirement age 60	Retirement age 65	Retirement age 70
	%	%	%
35	43	31	21
40	55	38	25
45	75	49	32
50	114	67	39
55	217	100	54
60	—	186	82

These rates are based on certain actuarial assumptions which may or may not be borne out in practice. Therefore, these contributions are really estimates of the likely future costs.

These contribution rates are calculated on certain assumptions regarding future increases in salary and investment return.

However, they do give an indication of the very significant amounts which a Company can inject into a Pension Fund for a controlling Director and write off in full for tax purposes. For example, a Director aged 55 with no previous Pension benefits could be included in a Scheme and the Company could contribute approximately twice his annual salary each year and receive full tax relief.

Of course, ultimately the benefits provided cannot exceed the Revenue maximum limits outlined in Chapter 5.

These contribution rates are considerably in excess of the 15% limit which applies to the self-employed under a Retirement Annuity Policy. Therefore, by and large, a Company Director who is not currently included in a Company Pension Arrangement would be much better off setting up such an arrangement rather than contributing on a personal basis to a Retirement Annuity.

It is often common to find that Company Directors with significant shareholdings do not draw a substantial taxable salary from the business. For Pension Scheme purposes, it should be remembered that benefits and contribution rates are based on income returnable and assessible to tax under Schedule E. Benefit-in-kind assessments in respect of subsidised loans and/or company cars can also be included in the definition of remuneration for Pension Scheme purposes.

6.3 RESTRICTIONS

While controlling Directors may now be included in Company Pension Schemes, some restrictions are placed on the benefits which may be provided for them. The two major restrictions are as follows:-

(1) *Definition of Final Remuneration:*
As pointed out in Chapter 5, the Revenue Commissioners allow, a choice of three definitions of final remuneration for Pension Scheme purposes. However, in the case of controlling Directors, the definition of final remuneration may only be based on one of these options — the average of total emoluments for any three or more consecutive years ending

not earlier than ten years before your normal retirement age. In other words, the definition of final remuneration as your remuneration at the date of retirement or shortly beforehand is not allowable in the case of controlling Directors.

(2) *Leaving the Company:*
In the case of a contributory Pension Scheme in which the controlling Director was included the Revenue Commissioners will not allow any refund of that Director's contribution to be made if he leaves the service of the Company unless his remuneration while a member of the Scheme was not in any year over £5,000.

6.4 "TOP HAT" SCHEMES

It may well be that as a company Director you are already included in the Company Pension Scheme along with the rest of your employees. If this Scheme does not, as is likely, provide the maximum approvable benefits, then it is always open to the Company to set up a special additional arrangement for its Directors and senior Executives — this type of arrangement is often referred to as a "Top Hat" Pension Scheme.

You can be included in more than one Pension Scheme with your employer provided the sum of the benefits provided under all of the Schemes does not exceed the maximum benefits outlined in Chapter 5.

6.5 MONEY PURCHASE ARRANGEMENTS

As pointed out in Chapter 5, many small Pension Schemes are arranged on a "money purchase" basis — that is where the benefits provided under the Plan are those secured by the contributions paid into it.

This type of arrangement is particularly common with small Schemes set up for one or two Directors. The Company can control its outlay and budget more accurately for it.

Money Purchase Arrangements are normally set up by way of individual Policies from Life Assurance Companies issued to the Pension Scheme Trustees in respect of each person covered in the Scheme. These Policies are virtually identical to the Retirement Annuities which were covered in Chapter 2.

The choice is the same as between Unit-Linked, With Profit

Endowment, and Deposit Account type Plans. The same type of factors, as discussed in Chapter 2, should be taken into account in making a choice between the various Plan types.

6.6 PORTABILITY

The right to carry your Pension benefits from one job to another can be very important. In this regard, a Money Purchase type Arrangement for a Directors Scheme usually includes automatic vested rights so that you are entitled to the benefit of contributions paid up to the date of leaving service. Because a Policy is often issued in respect of each individual included in the Plan, it may also be possible, if you leave service, to get your new employer to take up contributing to your existing Policy and hence continue your Pension Scheme funding.

It should be pointed out that the individual Policy is not issued to the member personally, but to the Trustee of the Scheme. The Trustee is usually the employer. Therefore, if you change employments, it may be possible for your first employer to assign the Policy over to your new employer as Trustee and hence continue the Policy unchanged. Of course you might not be able to get your new employer to contribute at the same rate as your previous employer.

6.7 SELF-ADMINISTERED SCHEMES

It is possible, as an alternative to using individual Pension Policies with Life Assurance Companies, for Directors to set up a small self-administered Scheme i.e. where the Trustees would control directly the investment of the Pension Scheme assets. In the case of a "small self-administered" Scheme the Revenue Commissioners have imposed some additional conditions of approval:

(1) **Appointment of a "Pensioneer Trustee"**
The Revenue insist that one of the Trustees must be a "Pensioneer Trustee" i.e. some outside person or body approved by the Revenue to ensure that the Scheme is run properly.

(2) **Investment of Fund Assets**
Certain investments are not allowed by the Revenue, such as

loans by the Fund to Directors, or acquiring any of the Company's assets. An exception might be allowed where a short term loan at *commercial rates of interest* is made to tide the Company over a period of financial difficulty where the absence of the loan might otherwise result in the failure of the Company.

6.8 DEATH BENEFITS

The same range of death benefits can be provided in a Scheme for a Director as outlined in Chapter 5. Again, if you are a Director and are included in more than one Scheme in respect of your employment, then the total of all the benefits payable on death cannot exceed the maximum levels.

6.9 SALARY SACRIFICE

Because of high rates of personal tax it may be more valuable, particularly if you are close to retirement, to forego salary increases in favour of the Company increasing its contribution to your Pension Plan.

For example, if you received an extra £1,000 per annum in salary, then the net benefit to you, after allowing for income tax at 60% and the Youth Employment Levy and Temporary Income Levy, is just £380.00 per annum.

If, on the other hand, the Company was to increase its contribution to your Pension Plan to the tune of £1,000 per annum, then the Company would be no worse off but your benefits would be boosted by this extra contribution of £1,000 per annum.

Of course if you do sacrifice the increase on your salary from the Company, then your Pension Benefits would be based on the lower taxable salary.

As an alternative, you could take the increase but put it directly into a top-up pension arrangement for yourself. Provided you don't contribute in total more than 15% of your earnings, the extra contribution will be fully allowed for tax purposes so that you will be no worse off, but your taxable income for pension purposes will be based on the higher figure.

6.10 SOCIAL WELFARE PENSION

If you are a majority shareholder and working Director, then you are probably paying P.R.S.I. at class K so that you would not be covered for any of the Social Insurance Pension benefits as outlined in Section III. This makes it all the more important to have a comprehensive Company Pension Scheme, if circumstances permit.

7. CIVIL SERVANTS

7.1 CIVIL SERVANTS

In this Chapter we cover the main Pension Scheme Benefits provided for "established" Civil Servants. The range of benefits described here apply broadly across the public sector but there are differences and, in particular, some semi-state Companies may operate their own separate Pension Schemes which do not provide exactly the level of the main Civil Service Scheme.

There is a separate Scheme for non-established State employees.

This Chapter covers the main Civil Service Pension Scheme which applies to the vast majority of permanent Civil Servants.

Strictly speaking, a Civil Servant is not automatically entitled to the various benefits outlined in this Chapter. Pensions are awarded as a result of satisfactory service completed. Therefore, any reference to being "entitled" to any benefits in this Chapter should be taken as being subject to this qualification.

7.2 YOUR BENEFITS

The main Civil Service Pension Scheme provides the following benefits for its Members:

- A Pension in retirement.
- An additional cash lump sum on retirement.
- A death gratuity.
- A marriage gratuity in some cases.

There is also an additional contributory spouses and childrens Pension Scheme which is a separate Arrangement.

7.3 WHAT PENSION WILL YOU RECEIVE IN RETIREMENT?

Provided you have at least five years reckonable service at retirement, you will be entitled to a Pension of 1/80th of your final pay for each year of reckonable service up to a maximum of 40/80ths or one-half of your final pay.

The retirement age for most Civil Servants is 65, and retirement with immediate payment after age 60 is allowed. However, special arrangements apply to certain grades of Civil Servants.

All paid full-time established service after age 16 in a Government department or office is treated as "reckonable service". Service is calculated by reference to completed days as well as completed years service.

Generally speaking your final pay is your basic pay on the last day of reckonable service. However, if you have been promoted or changed grades within the last three-years of service, then your pay may be averaged over the last three-year period for pension purposes.

7.4 WILL YOU RECEIVE A CASH LUMP SUM ON RETIREMENT?

Yes. *In addition* to your Pension you will be entitled, again assuming a minimum of five years reckonable service at retirement, to a cash lump sum of 3/80ths of your final pay for each year of service up to a maximum of 120/80ths or 1½ times your final pay. This lump sum is *in addition* to your Pension entitlements so that you do not have to commute or surrender any part of your Pension to obtain this lump sum.

However, a small number of female Civil Servants may be entitled to a pension based on 1/60th of final pay for each year of service with no cash lump sum entitlement.

Again as pointed out for the pension benefit above, retirement may take place at any time after age 60 and not later, normally, than age 65.

7.5 CAN YOU RETIRE EARLY DUE TO ILL HEALTH?

Yes. In the case of serious and permanent ill health, you may be entitled to retire early. Provided you have at least five years reckonable service, then on early retirement due to ill health, you will receive a Pension and cash lump sum as indicated above but based on your actual service completed to the date of ill health retirement plus "added service".

This added service is calculated on the following basis:-

(1) If you have between five and ten years actual service completed to the date of ill-health retirement, then you will be credited

with an equivalent amount of added service, subject to such credited service not being greater than the actual additional service which you would have completed if you had worked normally to age 65.

If, for example, you had 8 years service completed at the time of ill-health retirement, then you would receive credit for an additional 8 years provided you had at least 8 years potential service to age 65 at that stage.

(2) If you have more than ten years actual service completed to the date of ill-health retirement, then you will be credited with the more favourable of:

(a) The amount of service equal to the difference between your actual service completed and twenty years, and subject to such credited service not exceeding the additional service which you could have completed if you had worked normally to age 65 or

(b) 6 2/3rd years, again subject to such credited service not exceeding the additional service which you could have completed had you worked normally up to age 60.

Generally speaking, if you retire early on grounds of ill health after at least fourteen years service, your "added service" will be 6 2/3rd years.

Assuming that you joined the Civil Service at age 20 then this table shows your total reckonable service for pension and lump sum benefits on ill health retirement at various ages:-

Ill health retirement at age	Actual service completed	"Added service"	Total reckonable service
23	3	—	—*
30	10	10	20
35	15	6 2/3rds	21 2/3rds
40	20	6 2/3rds	26 2/3rds
45	25	6 2/3rds	31 2/3rds
50	30	6 2/3rds	36 2/3rds
55	35	5	40

*Minimum service of five years required.

This reckonable service would then be applied to calculate the appropriate ill health pension and cash lump sum.

Ill health retirement is not granted lightly and the Minister for the Public Service has to be "satisfied in the light of medical evidence that the person is incapable from infirmity of mind or body of discharging his duties and that the infirmity is likely to be *permanent*".

7.6 WHAT BENEFITS ARE PAYABLE ON DEATH IN SERVICE?

If you die while still in service, there is a lump sum benefit payable to your personal representatives. This lump sum is a gratuity amounting to the greater of a years pay at the date of death or the cash lump sum which would have been payable if you had retired on grounds of ill health on the date of death. This means that the lump sum payable will be at least equal to one years pay and up to but not exceeding 1½ years pay.

Generally speaking, where you have up to twenty years pensionable service completed at the date of death, then your lump sum death benefit will be 1 x salary.

Unlike the main retirement benefits, there is no minimum qualifying period of reckonable service for the lump sum death benefit.

If you are also a member of the separate contributory Spouses and Childrens Scheme, then pensions may become payable on your death to your widow or widower and children. See the separate paragraph later on in this chapter which covers this Scheme.

7.7 ARE THERE ANY BENEFITS PAYABLE ON DEATH IN RETIREMENT?

If at the time of your death, the total pension paid or payable since retirement, together with the cash lump sum, amounts to less than a years salary as at the date of retirement, then a gratuity sufficient to bring the total up to the equivalent of a years salary is payable to your personal representatives. Therefore, if you receive a retirement cash lump sum of greater than a years salary, there would obviously be no death gratuity subsequently payable on your death.

7.8 ALLOCATING YOUR PENSION

A pension may become payable to your spouse or other defined dependant if, at the date of your retirement, you had opted to "allocate" part of your pension in exchange for a dependants pension. You can allocate part of your pension in such a manner at the date of your retirement provided you are in good health.

Allocating part of your pension means that you give up part of your Pension now in exchange for a pension payable to your wife or other financial dependant in certain circumstances.

As far as providing a pension for your spouse is concerned, there are two options:-

(1) You could give up part of your pension in exchange for a pension for your spouse which would commence on your death, if your spouse was then living.

(2) Alternatively, you could give up part of your pension in exchange for an immediate pension payable to your spouse which would continue while both of you were alive and on your death, the amount of pension would double and continue to be paid to your surviving spouse for the rest of her lifetime. On the other hand, if your spouse pre-deceased you the pension would cease immediately.

The allocation of pension is made on the basis of certain factors and tables set out under the Superannuation Act 1956. The concept underlying these tables is that the pension which you give up is equal in value to the pension which you are providing for your spouse or dependants in certain circumstances.

Let us take an example. Let us say that you have reached your 60th birthday and you have decided to retire. Your final pensionable pay is £15,000 per annum and you have completed 40 years reckonable service. Your pension is therefore as follows:-

40/80ths x £15,000 = £7,500 per annum.

Your wife is aged 57 and you decide to allocate £2,000 per annum of your own pension in exchange for a pension for her to commence on your death if she is then living. The figures work out as follows:-

Your own pension before allocation	= £7,500 p.a.
Your reduced pension payable	= £5,500 p.a.
Your wife's pension (to commence on your death)	= £5,283 p.a.

You must make this allocation at the time of your retirement and you must be in good health and may possibly have to undergo a medical examination. You should also obviously not make such an allocation unless the named dependant is in good health. If for example, in the above case, your wife predeceased you, then the pension of £5,283 per annum does not obviously become payable while your own pension remains at £5,500 per annum.

Certain restrictions apply to the total amount of pension which may be allocated in this way.

7.9 WHAT HAPPENS IF YOU LEAVE THE CIVIL SERVICE?

If you leave the Civil Service voluntarily after at least five years service you would normally be entitled to a *reduced* pension and cash lump sum payable at age 60 in respect of your actual service completed.

For example, if you had completed eight years service and left the Civil Service voluntarily, then you would be entitled to a pension of 8/80ths of your remuneration and a cash lump sum of 24/80ths of your remuneration, payable at age 60.

These preserved benefits will be based on your actual service completed at the date of withdrawal and on your pensionable remuneration at the date of withdrawal but increased by reference to pension increases granted between your date of withdrawal and age 60.

Therefore, your preserved benefits will move in line with Civil Service Pension increases generally and should therefore be substantially protected against inflation.

If you are leaving the Civil Service and transferring to another public sector type employment then, in lieu of preserved benefits, you may be able to transfer your reckonable service into the Pension Scheme of your new employer. This is covered in more detail in the paragraph entitled "Transferability" later on.

Preserved pensions apply only if service cannot be transferred and no other benefit is payable.

7.10 DO YOU HAVE TO CONTRIBUTE TO THE PENSION SCHEME?

No. The main Civil Service Pension Scheme is non-contributory. However, if you are a member of the contributory Spouses and Childrens Pension Scheme you will have to contribute 1½% of your earnings to this Scheme.

7.11 CONTRIBUTORY SPOUSES AND CHILDRENS PENSION SCHEME

In addition to the main Scheme covered so far in this chapter, there is a separate contributory Spouses and Childrens Pension Scheme. This Scheme was originally established on the 1st January, 1969 and applied to all male Civil Servants who were appointed on or after the 1st January, 1969 and to those serving on that date who opted to become members of the Scheme. It also applied to female Civil Servants appointed on or after the 1st June, 1981 and to those already serving on that day who did not opt out of the Scheme. However, a new Scheme has been established on the 1st September, 1984. This new Scheme is covered in 7.12.

The benefits provided by the previous Scheme are as follows:

(1) If you die before retirement or in ill health retirement then your spouse will receive a pension of one half of your prospective pension, based on the total amount of pensionable service which you could have completed if you had worked normally to age 65. Therefore, if your total prospective service is forty years or more, your spouse would be entitled to a pension of one-quarter of your pensionable remuneration at the date of your death.

(2) If you die while in normal retirement, then your spouse will receive a pension of one-half of your pension.

(3) Where you leave children as well as a spouse then there is a children's pension payable equal to one-third of the spouse's pension for up to a maximum of three children. A childrens pension is payable until the child reaches age 16 or 21, if in full time education. If the child is permanently incapacitated by reason of mental or physical infirmity from maintaining himself or herself, then no age limit applies as long as he or she is incapable of maintaining himself or herself.

(4) Orphaned children are eligible for the pension which the spouse would have received had he/she lived, in the proportions of two-thirds of that pension for the first child and one-third for the second child. Again in the case of permanent invalidity, a child's pension will continue as long as the child is incapable of maintaining himself or herself. In the normal course of events, the orphans pension would cease at age 16 or 21 if in full time education.

This Scheme is contributory and you are required to contribute 1½% per annum of your pensionable remuneration. This contribution is payable from first becoming a member of the Scheme up to retirement or death, as the case may be.

Contributions are returnable in some circumstances:

a) Where you retire, resign or die and have had no spouse throughout the time you were included in the Scheme or

(b) You cease to be a Civil Servant in any circumstances other than death, where you do not qualify for a pension or preserved pension and your spouse is still alive.

Because this Scheme, on death before retirement or on ill-health retirement, gives credit for service completed up to age 65, there is a complicated procedure for a clawback from your retirement lump sum or death gratuity in respect of those years for which you have not contributed to the Scheme.

Any service reckonable in the calculation of Spouses and Childrens pensions which has not been paid for by way of the regular contribution during service is paid for at the rate of 1% p.a. of pensionable remuneration at the time of retirement or death.

For example, if you joined the Civil Service on the lst January, 1972 at age 20, then if you died at age 40 your actual completed service would be twenty years. However, your potential service to age 65 would have been 45 years but restricted to a maximum of 40 years for retirement benefit purposes. Therefore, on your death at age 40, your spouse would be entitled to a pension of half of your prospective pension based on your full service i.e

½ x 40/80ths x Salary = ¼ x Salary.

However, there would be a clawback from the death gratuity equal to 20% of salary in respect of the 20 years service, for which credit was given in the calculation of the widows pension, but for which period you had not contributed at the rate of 1½% per annum.

In lieu of the lump sum deductions you may opt to reduce that liability in advance by making an extra contribution at the rate of 1½% of salary for each year of reckonable service prior to entry to the Scheme. Income tax relief can be claimed on the periodic contributions up to a limit of 15% of your salary for each tax year.

7.12 NEW CONTRIBUTORY SPOUSES' & CHILDREN'S PENSION SCHEME

A new Scheme has been established on the 1st September, 1984. It applies to all Civil Servants appointed to established positions on or after lst September 1984 and to existing Civil Servants who opted to join the new Scheme on the lst September, 1984. The new Scheme widens the scope of dependants covered but restricts the circumstances in which a refund of contributions can be obtained.

A comparison of the difference between the two Schemes for a member is set out below:

Beneficiaries under new scheme	Beneficiaries under existing scheme
(1) Spouse of member, irrespective of date of marriage.	(1) Spouse of member, *if marriage takes place before retirement.*
(2) All legitimate children of member.	(2) Legimate children of member *if (a) conceived before retirement and (b) member was married during the period of contributing membership.*
(3) Illegitimate children of member.	(3) (Not covered).
(4) All step-children of member.	(4) step-children of member *if (a) member was married during the period of contributing membership and (b) member's marriage to child's parent takes place before retirement.*
(5) All adopted children of member	(5) Adopted children of member *if (a) member was married during the period of contributing membership and (b) child was adopted while member was married and (c) adoption takes place before retirement.*

7.13 INCREASES IN PENSIONS

Pensions are increased in line with general increases in Civil Servant salaries. However, pensions are also increased in line with any special increase in respect of the grade on which that pension was originally based. These grade increases in pensions are granted on the lst July each year.

7.14 TRANSFERRING SERVICE

If you leave the Civil Service and join some other public sector employment such as the Gardai, Defence Forces, Teachers, Universities, Local Authorities, Health Boards and most State sponsored bodies, then as an alternative to maintaining a deferred Pension with the Civil Service Pension Scheme, you may carry your service completed with the Civil Service into your new Pension Scheme.

Therefore, for example, if you left the Civil Service after ten years and joined one of these Public Sector bodies, the new Pension Scheme would give you credit for the ten years service already completed.

A similar system applies in the case of a transfer from a similar organisation into the Civil Service.

Generally speaking a credit in respect of transferred service would be treated for Pension, lump sum, and death benefit purposes as if it were actual service in the case of a transfer into the Civil Service.

7.15 PURCHASING ADDITIONAL YEARS SERVICE

Where you are likely to have less than the maximum of 40 years service by the time you reach age 60, then you may be able to purchase, at your own cost, additional years service. To be eligible to purchase additional years service you must have at at least nine years potential service to age 60.

Notional service may be purchased by one of two methods:-

(1) By periodical deductions from your salary up to age 60, or

(2) By lump sum payment.

You may opt to buy notional service by periodical deductions from your salary at any time in your career up to age 58. If you elect to buy service in this manner, then if you cease paying the periodic contributions the additional years service bought would be reduced proportionately. Contributions are normally payable from the date you decide to buy the additional service up to age 60.

The rates of contribution, expressed as a percentage of salary, for each year of notional service are set out in Appendix I for all ages.

As an alternative to purchasing the notional service by periodical deductions, it may be possible to purchase the notional service by a lump sum payment. This option must be exercised within two years of joining the Civil Service.

The lump sum contributions to purchase one year of notional service are set out in Appendix II.

The maximum amount of notional service which can be bought is set out in this Table:

Actual pensionable service (Including Transferred service but excluding notional service) which you would complete up to age 60	Maximum service which can be purchased
20 Years or More	40 - Actual Service to age 60
19	17
18	15
17	13
16	11
15	9
14	7
13	5
12	4
11	3
10	2
9	1

If you are entitled to retain benefits from another Occupational Pension Scheme then the maximum number of years of notional service which may be bought may be reduced to take account of these retained benefits.

Your contribution to purchase additional years service, either on a periodical or once off basis, will be allowed in full for income tax relief purposes up to 15% of your earnings in any tax year.

Under the Contributory Widows & Childrens Scheme, income tax relief is also available, within the overall 15% limit in any year, and this relief is automatically obtained by having the contribution deducted from your salary at source before income tax is levied. However, this procedure is not available in the case of periodical or lump sum contributions to purchase additional years service. In this case, you must claim the income tax relief direct from your Inspector of Taxes by way of an allowance on your P.A.Y.E. Certificate.

If you make a lump sum contribution and it exceeds 15% of your earnings for that tax year, then any excess may be carried forward into the following tax year and so on until the relief is granted in full.

The relief is available at your marginal rate of tax.

7.16 MARRIAGE GRATUITY

A Civil Servant who was serving on, or appointed from a competition advertised before 1st February, 1974 is eligible for a gratuity if, having given at least five years of reckonable service he/she resigns on marriage. The resignation must take place at the time of your marriage or within two years thereof.

The rate of gratuity is one months pay for each year of service, subject to a maximum of a years pay. Only service up to the date of marriage is reckonable and the gratuity is calculated on pay on that date or, if resignation takes place within two years after marriage, the then equivalent of that pay.

The marriage gratuity benefit now obviously applies to a declining number of Civil Servants and so is becoming less relevant as time progresses.

7.17 DISABILITY INSURANCE

One area in which the Civil Service Pension Scheme may not provide full coverage is in the area of prolonged disability or sickness. The ill-health pension provision of the Scheme would probably provide an ill-health pension of ¼ of your salary for people aged between 30 to 40. If therefore, you are a married man with family dependants, it would probably be wise to consider effecting some additional disability insurance along the lines outlined in Chapter 4. This is also advisable due to the fact that as an established Civil Servant, you would not be covered for any of the Social Welfare, sickness or disability benefits.

8. TOPPING-UP YOUR PENSION

8.1 EMPLOYEES

If you are an employee and are included already in your employers Pension Scheme, then you may be able to top-up your benefits at your own expense. You can do this by making an additional voluntary contribution to the Scheme — this type of arrangement is often referred to as an A.V.C. Arrangement.

The concept of the AVC Arrangement is that you set up your own personal Pension provision on top of your existing Scheme entitlements. The Revenue Commissioners have no objection to this provided that the total benefits which you receive from all Pension Schemes relating to your employment do not exceed the maximum benefits which were outlined in Chapter 5.

8.2 SCOPE FOR TOPPING-UP YOUR PENSION

You may only set up an Additional Voluntary Contribution Arrangement where you are already included in your employer's Pension Scheme. Therefore, an AVC arrangement must be *in addition* to your main Scheme benefits. The areas in which you may be able to top-up on your present benefits might be as follows:-

(1) *You may be entitled to less than the Revenue maximum pension benefits.*

For example, the maximum pension which your employer could provide you with, assuming you had at least ten years service at retirement age, would be 2/3rds of your final remuneration. However, your actual benefits may well be 1/60th of final remuneration for each year of service so that, for example, if you had service of twenty years at retirement, you may only be entitled to a pension of 20/60ths of final remuneration. The same points would apply in respect of the lump sum commutation option — which might be specified as 3/80ths of final remuneration for each year of service. Again, the maximum benefit is 1½ times salary after twenty years.

(2) *Some Schemes have their benefits integrated with Social Welfare Pension benefits as outlined in Chapter 5.*

You might, for example, be entitled to a Pension of 2/3rds of final pensionable remuneration with pensionable remuneration being defined as your actual salary less a deduction in respect of the Social Welfare Pension. However, the maximum Revenue limit is 2/3rds of your final actual remuneration so that you may have scope to provide an additional pension to bring you up to this maximum.

(3) *Your present Scheme may not provide you with the full benefits in respect of dependants' Pensions.*

For example, you may not be covered for a spouses pension on death in retirement. Again, you could contribute an additional amount to provide such a pension.

(4) *Your present pension benefits may not have any guaranteed increases built in.*

The Revenue rules say that Pensions in payment can increase in line with the cost of living. You could therefore, if your present Scheme did not allow for any increase in pension payments, contribute an additional amount in order to provide yourself with an increasing pension in retirement. The maximum rate of increase which the Revenue will allow you to anticipate in advance is 7½% per annum.

(5) *You may not be covered for maximum death-in-service benefits in your present Scheme.*

The maximum lump sum benefit is four times your remuneration at the date of death, together with a Spouses and Childrens Pension which in total may not exceed your total maximum prospective pension at the date of death. Many Schemes do not provide the maximum lump sum benefit of four times salary, so you may have scope to provide additional life assurance cover.

(6) *You may be able to pension remuneration which is not taken into account for your present Pension Scheme benefits.*

The type of earnings which are commonly not included in the main Pension Schemes include fluctuating bonuses and benefits in kind such as the charge relating to the use of a Company car and some loans from your employer at less than 12% per annum. In particular many people do not realise that they can provide pension benefits in respect of any benefit in kind assessments. BIKs are treated as taxable income by the Revenue Commissioners and hence can be included in the definition of remuneration for Pension Scheme purposes.

(7) *You may wish to retire earlier than the present retirement age in your Scheme.*

The Revenue's maximum limits allow you to retire early, on reduced benefits, from age 50 onwards. However, many Schemes would provide lower benefits on early retirement than the Revenue maximum allows.

8.3 HOW TO SET UP AN ADDITIONAL PENSION ARRANGEMENT

Your present Pension Scheme may already allow you to make Additional Voluntary Contributions. If this is so then you should contact your Employer regarding the arrangements to be made.

If your Pension Scheme does not allow for Additional Voluntary Contributions, then it may be possible to persuade your Employer to change the rules of the Scheme to allow for such contributions. Alternatively, with your Employer's consent, your Employer can set up an additional one-man Pension Scheme for yourself to which you contribute solely.

The usual arrangement in this case is for you to effect an individual Pension Policy with a Life Assurance Company along the lines of the Retirement Annuities set out in Chapter 2. In fact, the choice of policy is identical to the Retirement Annuities and reference should therefore be made to Chapter 2 for details of the type of Plans available.

Although you make the additional contribution entirely from your own funds, the Policy is actually issued to the Trustee of your Scheme which may well be your employer. This is so because legally, this is an *additional* Pension Arrangement, and the individual Policy which you effect is treated as an *additional* asset of the main Pension Scheme. However, the proceeds of that Policy can only be used for your benefit or for the benefit of your dependants.

It is normal where you effect an individual policy in such a manner that you will receive a copy of the policy but the original will be held by the Trustee of your main Pension Scheme.

8.4 INCOME TAX RELIEF

Any contribution to your AVC Arrangement is treated as a contribution to a Pension Scheme and is allowable within the overall

15% limit. This limit applies to the total of your contributions to the main Pension Scheme and to any AVC Arrangement.

Income tax relief is allowed at your marginal rate of tax in the year in which you make that payment.

In respect of an AVC Arrangement, the Revenue Commissioners insist that contributions once begun should be stopped only for good reason but in practice if they are made on a uniform basis in the expectation that they will continue for not less than five years (or until retirement if that is earlier) they may be allowed as ordinary annual contributions in the year in which they are paid.

AVC contributions may be restricted by the Revenue Commissioners if it is necessary to ensure that the total benefits received from your main Pension Scheme and the additional arrangement does not exceed the maximum benefits specified by the Revenue Commissioners.

If you are approaching retirement, then it may be possible to make a lump sum additional contribution now and have the tax relief allowed retrospectively for previous tax years up to 15% of earnings in each year up to a maximum of ten years in arrears. This is a very important point which should be borne in mind if you are very close to retirement. It can be an extremely tax efficient way of boosting your retirement benefits over a short period of time.

8.5 IF YOU LEAVE YOUR PRESENT EMPLOYMENT

If you leave your present employment and you had been contributing to an AVC Arrangement, then you may be entitled to a refund of your contributions, less tax at 10%, subject to the rules of your main Scheme permitting such a refund. However, in that case you would automatically forfeit any rights to a deferred pension in respect of your employer's contribution to the main Pension Scheme.

8.6 CIVIL SERVANTS

By and large, most established Civil Servants are well covered for Pension Scheme benefits. However, if you joined the Civil Service late in life you will not be entitled to the maximum benefits based on forty years reckonable service. However, in this case, it is likely that the arrangement to purchase additional years service with the Civil Service Pension Scheme, would be better value than setting up your own personal Additional Voluntary Contribution Arrangement. In addition, there is some doubt as to the legal validity of individual AVC Arrangements, using insurance policies, for members of the Civil Service.

III Social Welfare Pensions

We now turn to the various Pensions provided by the State under the Social Welfare system. These include Old Age, Invalidity and Dependants Pensions.

Pensions arise under the Social Welfare system from two separate Schemes:-

Social Insurance
Social Insurance Benefits are provided for employees who are insured under the Social Insurance Scheme. Entitlement to Pensions under this Scheme depends on having a certain number of qualifying contributions under the P.R.S.I. system at the appropriate rates. Benefits under this Scheme are *not* means tested.

Social Assistance
The Social Assistance Scheme provides pensions and benefits which are normally means tested. The Social Assistance Scheme applies to people who are not insured under the Social Insurance Scheme, or who have insufficient qualifying contributions to qualify for benefits under that Scheme or where their entitlement to certain benefits under the Social Insurance Scheme has terminated.

We will deal with the various Pensions arising under both these Schemes in turn. It should be remembered that these Pensions are designed to provide a basic level of income in retirement.

9. SOCIAL INSURANCE

9.1 INTRODUCTION

The Social Insurance Scheme provides various benefits, including Pensions, for insured employees. By and large, most employees aged 16 years of age and over must be covered by Pay Related Social Insurance, regardless of the level of their earnings. The Social Insurance Fund is financed by P.R.S.I. contributions from both the employee and the employer and by direct subvention by the Exchequer. Therefore, to be covered by the P.R.S.I. system, you need to be an employee.

Self-employed persons who have the equivalent of three years insurance as an employee, can in limited circumstances, make "voluntary" contributions to the Social Insurance Scheme for a limited range of benefits. However, the vast bulk of the self-employed and Company Directors with a majority shareholding in their company, would not be covered by the P.R.S.I. system for Pension benefits.

9.2 BENEFITS PROVIDED

A wide range of benefits is provided for insured employees under the P.R.S.I. system. There are different rates of contribution for employees depending on the nature of their employment and hence people are covered for varying level of benefits, depending on the rate of contribution which they pay. In this section of the book, we are concentrating on the Pension benefits provided by the P.R.S.I. system — the Retirement Pension, the Contributory Old Age Pension, the Contributory Widows Pension, the Contributory Orphans Allowance, and the Invalidity Pension.

9.3 P.R.S.I. CONTRIBUTION RATES

As pointed out above, different employees pay different rates of contribution, depending on the nature of their employment. The rate of contribution payable depends primarily on the contribution class into which you fall. The contribution classes range from class A to class N inclusive. Within a particular contribution class, there are three further sub-divisions indicated by the numbers 1, 2, 3. For example contribution class A is divided in A1, A2, and A3. The numbers 1, 2 and 3 represent different categories of persons. For example:

(1) Men and women insurable at the standard rate for their class.

(2) Women in receipt of certain Social Welfare benefits such as a Widows Pension, Deserted Wives Benefit, or Social Assistance Allowance.

(3) Men and women who hold medical cards.

The more important contribution classes and the employees covered in each case are as follows:-

Class A:
All persons in industrial, commercial and service type employment.

Class B:
Permanent and Pensionable Civil Servants.

Class C:
Gardaí and commissioned Army Officers.

Class D:
Permanent and pensionable employees of Local and Public Authorities or statutory transport undertakings and permanent and pensionable Teachers.

Class H:
Non-Commissioned Officers and enlisted Personnel of the Defence Forces.

Class J:
Persons insured for occupational injury and health purposes only. (This would include employed persons over age 66 or persons whose employment is of a subsidiary nature or of inconsiderable extent i.e. less than 18 hours a week).

Class K:
This applies to persons who are not insurably employed under the Social Welfare Acts, such as retired persons in receipt of occupational Pensions, certain Company Directors and Members of Religious Orders.

You can check which contribution class applies to you by checking your pay slip or your P60 which you should receive each year from your employer at the end of the tax year.

For most employees, P.R.S.I. contributions are collected through the P.A.Y.E. system. The main employee contribution rates for the particular classes set out above, are set out in detail in Appendix III.

People are often confused regarding the rate of P.R.S.I. which they must pay on their income. This is due to the fact that the P.R.S.I. contribution is in fact made up of a number of different components — the ordinary Social Insurance and Occupational

Injuries contribution, a contribution to the Redundancy and Employers Insolvency Fund, and three separate 1% charges the 1% Health Contribution, the 1% Youth Employment Levy and the 1% "Temporary" Income Levy payable on all income.

The basic P.R.S.I. contribution is payable on reckonable earnings which consist of your gross pay, less any pension contributions which are allowable for income tax purposes, up to a particular ceiling. For the tax year 1985/86, this ceiling is set at £13,800. The 1% Health contribution is payable on reckonable earnings up to a ceiling, which for 1985/86 is set at £13,000.

The 1% Youth Employment Levy and the 1% Temporary Income Levy apply to all income regardless of level. However, if you hold a medical card, your employer is liable to pay all three levies. If your pay for any week is less than £102, then your employer is liable to pay the 1% Income Levy on your behalf.

Therefore, the fact that these levies are collected through the P.R.S.I. system gives rise to the situation whereby people who are not insurable for Social Insurance Benefits can still pay what are technically P.R.S.I. contributions — for example Class K where people are not included for any Social Insurance Benefits, but make a contribution in respect of the Health, Youth Employment and Temporary Income Levy.

9.4 IF YOU ARE SELF-EMPLOYED

The Social Insurance Schemes basically apply only to employees. If you are self-employed you will normally not be covered by this Scheme. However, if you were employed and had only recently become self-employed, then it may be possible to make voluntary contributions to the Social Insurance Scheme in certain limited circumstances.

A person who ceased to be covered by compulsory Social Insurance (for example by becoming self-employed) can, if he is under age 66, opt to continue paying insurance on a voluntary basis for limited benefits, provided he has at least 156 weeks of insurable employment for which the appropriate employment contributions were paid while he was compulsory insured.

The amount of a voluntary contribution is calculated as a percentage of the contributor's reckonable income, which means income from any employment including any trade, business profession, office or vocation, up to a prescribed ceiling (£13,800 for 1985/86), in the preceding income tax year.

There are two rates of voluntary contribution:

(1) The full rate of 6.6% applies to persons who were compulsory insured for benefits which included Retirement and Old Age Pensions. Voluntary contributions at this 6.6% rate provide cover for Retirement Pension, Contributory Old Age Pension, Contributory Widows & Orphans Pension, Deserted Wives Benefit and Death Grant.

(2) A reduced rate of 2.6% applies to persons who are compulsorily insured in public service employment for limited benefits. Voluntary contributions at this 2.6% rate provide cover for Contributory Widows & Orphans Pension and Deserted Wives Benefit only.

Application to become a voluntary contributor must be made before the end of the income tax year following that in which compulsory insurance ceased.

If you are a married person, now self-employed, but are eligible to make the voluntary contribution, you should strongly consider doing so. This is particularly so if you are likely to qualify for the maximum rate of Retirement Pension and you feel that this Pension will continue to increase in line with the cost of living.

10. RETIREMENT PENSION

10.1 WHEN IS IT PAYABLE?

The Retirement Pension is payable to an insured person from age 65 onwards, provided certain conditions are satisfied.

10.2 WHO IS ENTITLED TO THIS PENSION?

To qualify for the Retirement Pension you must satisfy two basic conditions:-

(1) The retirement condition.

(2) The contribution conditions.

The Retirement Condition stipulates that at age 65 you must not engage in employment which is insurable under the Social Welfare Acts (other than employment which is insurable only for occupational injuries benefit). If therefore, you retired at age 65 and became self-employed, you would satisfy this Retirement Condition. The receipt of a Pension from your former employment would not contravene this Retirement Condition. On reaching age 66, the Retirement Condition ceases to apply and you are then free to engage in any employment.

The Contribution Conditions are quite complex and are set out in detail in Appendix IV. However, the three basic conditions, each of which must be fulfilled, are as follows:-

(1) You must have started paying contributions before you were 55 years of age.

(2) You must have at least 156 contribution weeks of insurable employment for which the appropriate contributions have been paid.

(3) You must have a yearly average of at least 24 contribution weeks over a particular period. The period in question is broadly from 1953 (or a later year if you first became insured after 1953) up to the last full insurance year before your 65th birthday.

It is this third condition which can cause problems for some people. It can be a disadvantage to have an insurance record going back a fairly long period. The higher the number of years since you were first insured, the lower will be your average yearly contribution, especially if you had a broken record of contributions.

An interesting point to note is that if you have been insured in another member state of the E.E.C. as well as in this Country, your insurance record in that other state can be taken into account when deciding whether you are eligible or not for a Retirement Pension.

However, not everybody insured under the P.R.S.I. system is entitled to a Retirement Pension. The classes of contribution which provide for the Retirement Pension include class A, E, F, G, H, and N. Employees who are not entitled to the Retirement Pension would include permanent and pensionable employees in the Civil Service, Gardaí, Commissioned Army Officers, and Teachers.

10.3 HOW MUCH IS PAYABLE?

The amount payable is comprised of three separate elements —

a personal amount payable to you, an adult dependant supplement, and a child dependant supplement, which is normally only payable for children under 18 years of age. An adult dependant would in the case of a married man, include his wife if she is living with him or is wholly or mainly maintained by him or in the case of a married woman, would include her husband if he is an invalid and is wholly or mainly maintained by her.

However, the Social Welfare (Amendment) (No. 2) Bill 1984, which is currently (May, 1985) before the Dail would have a major impact on the definition of an "adult dependant". Under the proposed new definition, an "adult dependant" will reflect the actual state of affairs — in other words, actual financial dependancy will be the criterion.

Under the new rules, a spouse may be an adult dependant if he/she is being wholly or mainly maintained by the social welfare pensioner and is *not* in employment or self-employed, or receiving any social welfare benefit.

However, under this new definition, some married men may lose the adult dependant allowance for their wife, if she has an independant source of income.

This table sets out the main rates of benefit payable from July, 1985 in respect of the Retirement Pension:-

Retirement pension — July 1985 weekly benefits

Maximum Personal Rate	—	Under 80	£51.40
	—	80 or over	£54.90
Increase for *adult dependant*	—	under 66	£32.80
Increase for *adult dependant*	—	age 66 or over	£38.35
Increase for Children	—	First child	£10.60
		Second child	£11.70
		Third to fifth child	£ 9.75
		Sixth and subsequent children	£ 8.00
Living alone allowance for pensioner age 66			£ 3.40

The *personal* rate of pension depends on your yearly average number of contributions [see condition C (in Appendix IV)]. A yearly average of 48 is required for the maximum rate and 24 for the minimum level. The supplements for dependants are payable in full whether you are entitled to the maximum or reduced personal rates.

Therefore, a married man and his wife both over age 66, would currently receive a maximum total Retirement Pension of £89.75p assuming that they had no dependant children.

In recent years, successive Governments have pledged themselves to at least maintain the real value of Social Welfare benefits. Consequently, benefits such as the Retirement Pension have tended to increase in line with the cost of living year by year. In fact, over the last few years, the rate of benefit has increased faster than the cost of living, as this graph shows.

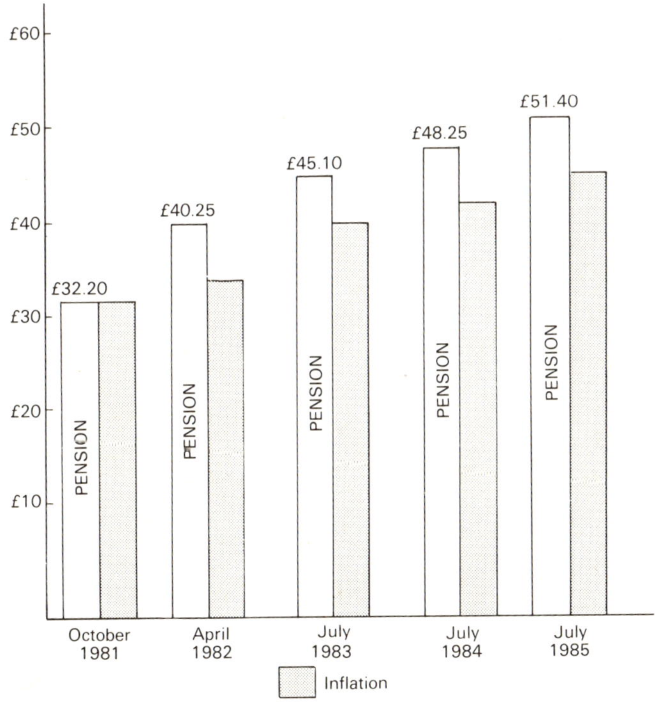

It should be remembered that there is currently no pay related element attaching to the Retirement Pension or indeed any of the other Pensions under the Social Insurance Scheme.

10.4 WHAT HAPPENS IF YOU DIE?

If you die while you are in receipt of a Retirement Pension, your spouse would be eligible to continue to receive the Retirement Pension for six weeks after your death. Then if your Pension had included an increase in respect of your wife, your widow will be entitled to a contributory Widow's Pension at the maximum rate. On the other hand, if your pension had included an increase in respect of your invalid husband, on your death he would be entitled to a Survivors benefit at the same rate as the maximum contributory Widow's Pension.

10.5 IS THE PENSION LIABLE TO TAX?

Yes. The Retirement Pension, the Old Age Contributory Pension, the Widows Contributory Pension, the Orphans Contributory Allowance and the Invalidity Pension are all liable to income tax where they have been received for more than one year. However, tax is not deducted at source, as most of these Pensions are payable by way of pension books, with pension orders which may be cashed at the Post Office. The amount of a Retirement Pension should be included with the rest of your taxable income in assessing your income tax liability for a particular year. However, for people who are likely to have little other income other than the Retirement Pension, it is unlikely that any income tax will be payable.

There is an age income tax exemption limit of £3,000 for persons aged 65 years or over and £3,500 for persons aged 75 years or over. These limits are doubled for married couples. Therefore, in the case of a married couple aged 65 years or over, the exemption limit would be £6,000. These exemption limits would normally more than cover the Retirement Pension with adult dependant supplements.

For example, the Retirement Pension payable to a married couple both aged over 66, is £89.75 per week, which would be underneath the £6,000 income tax exemption limit. However, if you are also entitled to a Pension from your employment or from some other source, then the combined Pensions could well push you above the general exemption limit and hence a liability to income tax will arise. Of course, in that case you would be entitled to the various personal allowances available to income tax payers. A full set of these allowances, together with income tax bands is set out in Appendix V.

10.6 CONTRIBUTORY OLD AGE PENSION

The contributory Old Age Pension is considered in more detail in the next chapter. However, there is often confusion between the Retirement Pension and the contributory Old Age Pension as the maximum rate of benefit is the same for both Pensions. A person receiving a reduced rate of Retirement Pension may possibly qualify for a higher rate contributory Old Age Pension at age 66. In that case, your Retirement Pension would cease at age 66 and you could then claim the higher contributory Old Age Pension.

If you are awarded a contributory Old Age Pension payment of the Retirement Pension will cease. It is not possible to claim both Pensions. The contributory Old Age Pension starts at age 66, while the Retirement Pension is payable from age 65. If you intend to retire at age 65, then it would be possible, if you qualify for the maximum rate of benefit, to claim the Retirement Pension from age 65 onwards without any need to change to a contributory Old Age Pension as the maximum rate of benefit would be the same in both cases.

However, many people who retire at age 65 choose to register as unemployed for the year between age 65 and 66, so that they might receive unemployment benefit together with the pay-related supplement for that year. Of course, you must qualify for the unemployment benefit and you must be available for work during that year to claim it. Then at age 66 you may qualify for the contributory Old Age Pension.

Many people choose to claim unemployment benefit rather than claim the Retirement Pension, due to the fact that the payment of the pay-related supplement, together with the basic rate of benefit is likely to exceed the maximum rate which they could claim under the Retirement Pension. In addition, the unemployment benefit and pay-related supplement would not be liable to tax whereas the Retirement Pension would be.

11. CONTRIBUTORY OLD AGE PENSION

11.1 WHEN IS THE PENSION PAYABLE

The Contributory Old Age Pension is payable to an insured person from age 66 onwards, if he satisfies the contribution conditions. Your right to this Pension is not affected by any Pension that you might have from your former employment nor is it necessary to actually retire to qualify for it.

11.2 WHO IS ENTITLED TO THIS PENSION?

Basically the same P.R.S.I. contribution classes which were outlined for the Retirement Pension in the previous chapter are also eligible to claim the contributory Old Age Pension. This means that permanent and pensionable Civil Servants, Gardaí, Commissioned Army Officers, and other Public Service workers would not be entitled to the contributory Old Age Pension.

It is not possible to claim both Pensions — you may claim one or other, but not both. To qualify for the contributory Old Age Pension, you must satisfy three separate contribution conditions which are set out in some detail in Appendix VI. The three contribution conditions are briefly as follows:-

(1) You must have become insured before age 56 if born on or after the lst October, 1922. Higher age limits apply if you were born before the lst October, 1922.

(2) You must have at least 156 qualifying contributions paid in respect of your employment.

(3) You must have a yearly average of at least 20 paid or credited contributions over the period from 1953 or year of entry into insurance (whichever is the later) to the end of the last complete contribution year before you attained Pension age.

As pointed out in Chapter 10 for the Retirement Pension, it is this third condition which often causes problems for people trying to qualify for a contributory pension.

11.3 WHAT LEVEL OF BENEFIT IS PAYABLE?

The rates of benefit set out in the previous chapter for Retirement Pension are precisely the same for the Old Age Contributory Pension. The maximum personal rate is the same in both cases at £51.40 per week for a Pensioner under age 80 and at £54.90 per week for a Pensioner over age 80. The comments made in Chapter 10 with regard to the new definition of adult dependants also apply to the Contributory Old Age Pension. Because of differing contribution conditions, it is possible that you might qualify for a higher rate of contributory Old Age Pension than Retirement Pension.

In this case, if you are in receipt of the Retirement Pension at age 66, the Department of Social Welfare will automatically examine your case and if it is to your benefit will change your Pension to the higher Contributory Old Age Pension.

11.4 IS THE PENSION LIABLE TO INCOME TAX?

Yes. As pointed out in the previous chapter, most Social Insurance Pension benefits are liable to income tax. However, tax is not deducted at source and a tax liability would probably not arise if this Pension was to be your only source of income. The general exemption and age exemption limits for income tax are set out in Appendix V. These limits would more than cover the normal maximum rate of Retirement or Contributory Old Age Pension. However, if you are in receipt of additional taxable income, then the combination of both might mean that you will end up paying tax.

11.5 WHAT HAPPENS IF YOU DIE?

If you die while in receipt of a Contributory Old Age Pension, then a very similar position applies as outlined in the case of the Retirement Pension. In other words, your dependant spouse will receive your Pension for six weeks after your death. Then if your Pension included an allowance in respect of your spouse, your surviving widow is automatically entitled to a Contributory Widow's Pension at the maximum rate. Similarly, if your pension had included an allowance in respect of your invalid husband, then on your death he would be entitled to a Survivor's Benefit at the same rate as the maximum contributory Widow's Pension.

12. CONTRIBUTORY WIDOW'S PENSION

12.1 WHEN IS THE PENSION PAYABLE?

The contributory Widow's Pension is payable to a widow, regardless of her age, on the death of her husband if the contribution conditions are satisfied on either her late husband's insurance or on her own insurance record at the date of her husband's death. On the death of a Retirement Pensioner or a contributory Old Age Pensioner, whose pension included an allowance in respect of his wife, the surviving widow is also automatically entitled to a contributory Widow's Pension at the maximum rate.

at least 26 contribution weeks of insurable employment for which the appropriate contributions have been paid or registered for that orphan's parent or step-parent. The P.R.S.I. contribution classes covered for the contributory Orphan's Allowance are the same as for the contributory Widow's Pension covered in the previous chapter. Therefore, virtually all employees, both public and private sector, are covered for this benefit.

13.3 WHAT LEVEL OF BENEFIT IS PAYABLE?

The current weekly rate of Orphan's Contributory Allowance is £29.25 as and from July, 1985. This allowance is ordinarily payable until the orphan reaches age 18 or age 21 if in full-time education.

13.4 IS THE ALLOWANCE LIABLE TO INCOME TAX?

Yes. The allowance is treated as the child's income and is liable to income tax.

14. INVALIDITY PENSION

14.1 WHEN IS INVALIDITY PENSION PAYABLE?

Invalidity Pension is payable to an insured person when he or she becomes *permanently* incapable of work due to sickness or disability.

14.2 WHO IS ENTITLED TO AN INVALIDITY PENSION?

To qualify for an Invalidity Pension, you must have been insured at the appropriate contribution class and:-

(1) be permanently incapable of work and

(2) satisfy the contribution conditions.

Those who qualify for Pension will normally be persons satisfying the contribution conditions who have been receiving short-term disability benefit under the Social Insurance Scheme for a continuous period of at least twelve months and are likely to be permanently incapacitated. It is not possible to claim both Invalidity Pension and Disability Benefit — only one of them may be claimed at the same time.

Not all P.R.S.I. contribution classes are covered for Invalidity Pension. The contribution classes which are covered for Invalidity Pension are — classes A, E, F, G, H, and N. The people excluded are permanent pensionable civil servants and others in the public service, such as Gardaí and Teachers, who are entitled to sick pay or an ill-health pension under the conditions of their employment.

The contribution conditions which must be satisfied to successfully claim an Invalidity Pension are:-

(1) You must have had not less than 156 contribution weeks of insurable employment for which the appropriate contributions have been paid, and

(2) You must have not less than 48 contribution weeks registered in the contribution year immediately before you became permanently incapable of work.

14.3 WHAT LEVEL OF BENEFIT IS PAYABLE?

The level of Invalidity Pension payable from July 1985 is as follows:-

Invalidity pension

Weekly rates July 1985

	Under 66 £ p.w.	66 or over £ p.w.
Maximum Personal Rate	45.30	46.20
Increases for Dependants:		
Adult	29.40	30.00
First child	10.45	10.60
Second child	11.50	11.70
Third to fifth child	9.55	9.75
Sixth & subsequent children	7.75	8.00
Maximum personal rate for a married woman dependant upon her husband	39.90	40.60
Living alone allowance for Pensioner over 66		3.40

The maximum personal rate shown above is payable in respect of a man, single woman or widow, not receiving a Widow's

Pension, married woman living apart from and unable to obtain any financial assistance from her husband, or a married woman entitled to an increase in respect of a child dependant or for an adult dependant. Therefore, in the case of a married woman who would not fall within any of the above categories, the lower maximum personal rate indicated — £39.90 per week under age 66 — would normally be payable.

The increase for an adult dependant would normally apply in the case of a married man where his wife is living with him or is wholly or mainly maintained by him. In the case of a married woman, her husband is a qualified adult dependant if he is an invalid and is wholly or mainly maintained by her.

In the normal course of events, children would be qualified dependants of their father. However, children may be qualified dependants of their mother where she would be entitled to an adult dependant's allowance in respect of her invalid husband or if her husband is not living with her and is not wholly or mainly supporting her. The age limit for a qualified child dependant is normally 18 years of age except where a widow is claiming the Invalidity Pension and the children are receiving full-time education, in which case the upper age limit of 21 years applies.

However, the Social Welfare (Amendment) (No. 2) Bill 1984 would make major changes in the following areas, if passed by the Dáil:

(1) A married woman, dependant upon her husband would be entitled to the same rate of benefit as a man — i.e. £45.30 as opposed to the present maximum rate of £39.90.

(2) As pointed out in Chapter 10, the definition of adult dependant will be altered and will include a married man financially dependent upon his wife.

(3) Children will be regarded as the dependants of either parent, depending on the family circumstances. For example, if the woman is the only breadwinner, she will be entitled to claim the Child Dependant allowance for the children.

The Invalidity Pension is payable only as long as you remain permanently incapable of work or until you become entitled to a Retirement or Old Age Pension. Invalidity Pension is not payable at the same time as certain other Social Welfare benefits in respect of the same period.

14.4 IS THE INVALIDITY PENSION LIABLE TO INCOME TAX?

Yes. The Invalidity Pension is liable to tax.

14.5 WHAT HAPPENS IF YOU DIE?

If you die while in receipt of an Invalidity Pension, then payment of the benefit ceases and your dependants at that stage may become entitled to a contributory Widow's Pension or a contributory Orphan's Allowance, as the case may be.

15. SOCIAL ASSISTANCE SCHEMES

15.1 INTRODUCTION

Social Assistance differs from Social Insurance in that entitlement to Social Assistance benefits depends entirely on a means test. Entitlement to Social Insurance benefits depends on an individual being an insured person, in other words paying P.R.S.I. contributions. Every person is entitled to benefit under Social Assistance Schemes provided they satisfy the means test involved.

Social Assistance Schemes are financed entirely from the Exchequer, as opposed to the Social Insurance benefits which are financed partly by the employers' contributions, employees' contributions, and a subvention from the Exchequer.

Social Assistance Schemes cover the following categories of people:-

(1) People who are not included within the Social Insurance Scheme, which would be mainly people who are not in employment.

(2) People who are included in the Social Insurance Scheme, but have insufficient contributions to qualify for certain Social Insurance benefits — for example, people who fail to qualify for unemployment benefit might qualify for unemployment assistance under the Social Assistance Scheme.

(3) People who have exhausted their entitlement to Social Insurance benefits. Again, for example somebody might claim unemployment benefit, together with pay related benefit under the Social Insurance Scheme until such time as entitlement to

that would expire. At that stage, you could then apply for unemployment assistance under the Social Assistance Schemes.

The main point to remember about Social Assistance Schemes is that they are designed for the least well-off sections of the community — they are in a sense a last resort after all other benefits and entitlements have ceased.

16. NON-CONTRIBUTORY OLD AGE PENSION

16.1 WHEN IS THE PENSION PAYABLE?

The non-contributory Old Age Pension is payable from age 66 onwards.

16.2 WHO IS ENTITLED TO CLAIM THIS PENSION?

The non-contributory Old Age Pension is one of the most "popular" Social Welfare benefits, with an estimated 127,371 people claiming the non-contributory Old Age Pension at the 30th June, 1984, compared with 72,289 for the Old Age Contributory Pension and 33,483 for the Retirement Pension. You are entitled to claim the non-contributory Old Age Pension provided you:

(1) Are aged 66 years or over.

(2) Are ordinarily resident in the State.

(3) And satisfy a means test.

The procedure involved in the means test is that when you apply for a non-contributory Old Age Pension, a Social Welfare Officer will investigate your claim at your home. He will conduct the means test. The Officer then reports the results of his investigation to the deciding office in the Department of Social Welfare, who decides the claim. The Deciding Officer's decision is final unless an appeal is made against it within a certain time.

16.2 MEANS TEST

In assessing what rate of Pension, if any, a person is entitled to the Social Welfare Officer will determine your "weekly means". Where your weekly means do no exceed a current limit of £6.00 per week, then the maximum rate of Pension is payable.

16.3 HOW ARE YOUR "WEEKLY MEANS" CALCULATED?

In asscssing a pcrsons mcans, a Social Welfare Officer will take account of:-

(1) Any income which you might reasonably expect to receive during the following year,

(2) the value of any investments and capital held and the value of any property not personally used, for example, a second home, and

(3) the value of any property personally used by you such as a farm but *not* your own home.

Certain items of income are *not* taken into account when assessing your weekly means. A full list of these items which are excluded, together with a more detailed note on the calculation of means, is set out on Appendix VIII.

Confusion often arises regarding what level of investments and capital you may hold while still qualifying for a non-contributory Old Age Pension. The actual income from investments or money in a Savings Account is *not* taken as the means.

Instead, an estimated yearly cash value is put on investments or property. This estimated yearly cash value is calculated by excluding the first £200 in value, taking 5% of the next £375, and 10% of the balance. This yearly cash value is then added to any cash on hands or balance in a current Bank Account. The total is divided by 52 to arrive at the weekly means value. If the weekly value is £1.00 or more, the weekly means are taken to be the weekly value plus £1.00.

For example, the weekly means of an individual with £3,000, say, invested in a Building Society account and no other income or assets might be calculated as follows:-

The first £200.00 is excluded,
The next £375.00 is taken at 5% i.e. £18.75,
The balance of £2,425 is taken at 10% — i.e. £242.50.

The total estimated cash value is therefore £261.25 or £5.02 per week. The weekly means is therefore taken as this amount plus £1.00 — £6.02 per week.

This means test is seen by some people as being unfair now that interest rates have fallen to much lower levels than prevailed in recent times. For example, in the above example the assumed income from the £3,000 Building Society Account is taken as £261.25 p.a., while current interest rates of 7% p.a. would only produce an actual income of £210.00 p.a.

In calculating the means of a married individual, means are taken at one-half of the total means of the married couple.

An obvious loop-hole, particularly with the farming community, was for an individual approaching age 66 to transfer most if not all of his or her property to a son or daughter. The objective was to severely reduce the assessible ''weekly means'', so as to qualify for the maximum rate of Pension.

However, if a person transfers property or income for the sole purpose of qualifying for a Pension, the transfer is ignored in calculating his or her means for Pension purposes, except where the assignment is that of a farm to a child or children of the person assigning it and where the ratable value, including buildings, does not exceed £30.00. It is also required that, in this case, the person transferring the farm should not have been the owner or occupier of lands exceeding that ratable value in the three years preceding the date of the claimed Pension.

16.4 WHAT LEVEL OF BENEFIT IS PAYABLE?

The maximum personal rate of Pension is payable where weekly means do not exceed £6.00. No personal rate of Pension is payable where weekly means exceed £48.00. In between there is a sliding scale which is set out in full in Appendix IX. The maximum personal rates as and from July, 1985 are as follows:-

Old age non-contributory pension
Maximum personal rates — July 1985

	Under 80 £ p.w.	Over 80 £ p.w.
Personal Rate	44.00	47.20
Person with adult dependant under 66	66.10	69.30

Of course, where both Pensioners are aged 66 or over and qualify separately for the Old Age non-contributory Pension, then each is entitled to the maximum rate of £44.00, if under age 80. An adult dependant will be basically the wife of a Pensioner, provided she herself is not in receipt of a Social Welfare Pension or allowance, and the husband of a Pensioner provided she is wholly or mainly maintaining him and he is incapacitated and is not receiving any Social Welfare Pension.

However, the comments in Chapter 10 regarding the proposed altering of the definition of adult dependant would apply to this pension also.

16.5 IS THE PENSION LIABLE TO INCOME TAX?

No. Social Assistance benefits are not liable to income tax as generally speaking, they are means tested and therefore anybody who would be entitled to receive, for example, the non-contributory Old Age Pension should not be liable to income tax in any event.

16.6 WHAT HAPPENS IF YOU DIE?

If you die while in receipt of a non-contributory Old Age Pension, and leave an adult dependant such as your wife, or in the case of a woman her incapacitated husband, then the Pension will continue to be paid to that adult dependant for a period of six weeks after the date of death. Thereafter, benefit ceases. In the case of a wife who is an adult dependant, the non-contributory Widow's Pension may then be payable.

17. NON-CONTRIBUTORY WIDOW'S PENSION

17.1 WHEN IS THE PENSION PAYABLE?

The non-contributory Widow's Pension is payable to a woman on the death of her husband, provided she is not entitled to the contributory Widow's Pension and can satisfy a means test.

17.2 WHO IS ENTITLED TO CLAIM THIS PENSION?

The non-contributory Widow's Pension is payable to a widow as long as she remains a widow, satisfies the means test, and remains in the State.

17.3 MEANS TEST

The procedure for assessing the weekly means is very similar to that outlined in the previous chapter for the non-contributory Old Age Pension. However, there are two differences in the case of the non-contributory Widow's Pension which should be noted:-

(1) In calculating "weekly means" a widow is allowed to earn £312.00 a year for each dependant child. For example, a widow with three dependant children (deemed to be children under age 18 or 21 if in receipt of full-time education), could earn £936.00 per annum or £18.00 per week, which would not be assessed as means.

(2) In assessing the yearly cash value of any investments or property belonging to but not personally used by the widow, the rules are as follows:-

The yearly value is calculated by excluding the first £200 and, if there are dependant children, a further £100 for each dependant child, and taking 5% of the balance. The yearly value thus arrived at is divided by 52 to arrive at the weekly value. If the weekly value is £1.00 or more, the weekly means are taken to be the weekly value plus £1.00. Again, for example, in the case of a widow with three dependant children the first £500.00 of value would be ignored with 5% of the balance being taken as the yearly cash value.

17.4 WHAT LEVEL OF BENEFIT IS PAYABLE?

The maximum personal rate of benefit is payable where the assessed weekly means do not exceed £6.00. No benefit is payable where the assessed weekly means exceed £48.00. In between a sliding scale applies and this is set out fully in Appendix X.

Maximum personal rates, together with the supplements for dependant children are set out in the table opposite.

17.5 IS THE PENSION LIABLE TO INCOME TAX?

No. As for the Old Age non-Contributory Pension, Social Assistance Benefits are not liable to income tax.

17.6 WHAT HAPPENS IF YOU DIE?

If you die while in receipt of a Widow's non-contributory Pension then payment of the Pension obviously ceases but any child dependants may be entitled to a non-contributory Orphan's Pension at that stage.

Non-contributory widow's pension
Maximum rates — July 1985

	Pensioner under 66 £ p.w.	Pensioner over 66 £ p.w.
Personal Rate	43.15	48.00*
Increases for Children:		
— First	11.25	11.50
— Second to fifth	12.35	12.65
— Sixth and subsequent	10.60	10.80

*If 80 or over, then supplement of £3.20 applies.

18. NON-CONTRIBUTORY ORPHAN'S PENSION

18.1 WHEN IS THIS PENSION PAYABLE?

A non-contributory Orphan's Pension may become payable when a child is orphaned.

18.2 WHO IS ENTITLED TO THIS PENSION?

A non-contributory Orphan's Pension is payable in respect of an orphan who satisfies a means test and in respect of whom a contributory orphan'a allowance is not payable.

18.3 MEANS TEST

The means test is similar to that set out for the non-contributory Old Age Pension in Chapter 16. An orphan is basically a legitimate child both of whose parents are dead or an illegitimate child whose mother is dead and whose father is dead or unknown, or a child whose father or mother has died and who has been deserted or abandoned by the other parent.

18.4 WHAT LEVEL OF BENEFIT IS PAYABLE?

The maximum personal rate in respect of each orphan is currently £24.50 per week. This maximum rate is payable where the assessed weekly means do not exceed £1.00. Where the assessed weekly means exceed £23.00 no benefit is payable. In between a sliding scale applies and this scale is set out fully in Appendix XI.

18.5 IS THE PENSION LIABLE TO INCOME TAX?
No. As with other Social Assistance benefits, this Pension is not liable to income tax.

18.6 WHEN DOES THE PENSION CEASE?
The Pension is payable until the orphan reaches age 18 or 21, if he is in full-time education as long as the means test is satisfied throughout. Benefit will normally be paid to the orphan's guardian.

IV Providing for Additional Retirement Income

In this final section of the book, we deal with some other ways to provide an income in retirement. These are personal arrangements which are open to most people and would not in any way affect or be affected by any Personal Pension Policy or Company Pension Scheme benefits to which you might be entitled.

19. ALTERNATIVES

19.1 PERSONAL ANNUITIES

In this section of the book we are looking at ways in which you can provide a regular income for yourself outside of any personal or company Pension Arrangement or social welfare benefits.

Most of the options covered involve the investment of a lump sum to produce a regular income.

19.2 NEST EGG

Even if you are already included in a Pension Arrangement, either on a personal basis or as a member of a Company Pension Scheme, it is very likely that you are also putting money aside on a regular basis to build up a "nest egg" for your retirement. For example, you may be contributing to a Life Assurance Savings Plan or National Instalment Saving or simply putting money in a Bank or Building Society on a regular basis.

Because this lump sum is not tied in with any Pension Arrangement, it is not subject to any restrictions or conditions as to what use you put it to. You therefore have a wide choice of ways in which to use this nest egg to provide an income for yourself and your dependants in retirement. On retirement you may also be entitled to a substantial tax-free lump sum from your Pension Scheme. This amount may also be available for investment. In this section of the book, we cover some of these options available.

20. PURCHASED LIFE ANNUITIES

20.1 PURCHASED LIFE ANNUITIES

A Purchased Life Annuity is a personal annuity which you can buy from any Life Assurance Company on a voluntary basis. In other words, the annuity is not related to any Pension Scheme and is a personal arrangement.

An annuity has often been described as the reverse of a Life Assurance Policy. Under a conventional Life Assurance Plan you pay a small regular premium to the Life Office in return for a capital sum on your death for your next of kin.

However, in the case of a personal annuity, you pay a lump sum now to the Life Office and in return they pay you a regular income for an agreed period, such as for your lifetime. On your death, the annuity ceases and no capital sum, generally speaking, is payable.

Therefore, it should be appreciated straight away that you should not consider purchasing a personal annuity unless you are currently in good health and have a normal expectation of life.

20.2 DIFFERENT TYPES OF ANNUITIES

The different types of annuities which you can purchase are similar to those outlined in the case of the Retirement Annuities under Chapter 2.

Some of the variations in annuities include:

(1) You can purchase an annuity for a temporary period, such as ten or fifteen years, or the annuity can be payable for life or for the joint lives of yourself and your spouse.

(2) The annuity can be payable at different frequencies — such as monthly, half-yearly, or yearly.

(3) The annuity can be a level one or escalating at some rate such as 5% per annum.

(4) The annuity can be guaranteed to be paid for a certain minimum period whether or not you survive — for example, a guaranteed minimum period of five years is common.

(5) It is also possible to buy what is called a "capital protected annuity". This is a form of annuity whereby on your death,

the difference between the sum which you invested in the total annuity and the annuity payments which you had already received is returned to your estate as a lump sum.

(6) You can purchase a joint-life annuity which will continue to be paid while either yourself or your spouse is alive.

20.3 INCOME TAX AND PURCHASED LIFE ANNUITIES

In its simplest form, purchasing an annuity involves investing a capital sum now with a Life Assurance Company in return for a regular income. In a sense, once you invest your lump sum with the Life Assurance Company, it is lost because you cannot recover it entirely.

Therefore, the annuity which the Life Office pays you represents partly a return of your capital sum invested and partly the investment income which that office can make on the sum invested with them.

Therefore, from an income tax point of view, part of the income which you receive should really be treated as a return of your capital and not taxed as income.

This principle has been recognised since 1959 and Section 239 of the Income Tax Act 1967 provides for what is often called a "capital content" element of the annuity. In other words, the capital content part of the annuity payment is not liable to income tax, whereas the balance is.

20.4 ANNUITY RATES

The annuity which any particular Life Office will grant you in return for a lump sum investment will vary from time to time in line with interest rates. Life Assurance Companies match their annuity rates closely with the types of returns which they in turn can obtain on Government Securities.

However, once you purchase your annuity, the particular rate is fixed and cannot be varied by the Life Office thereafter.

Annuity rates are often expressed as the annual income which can be provided by a lump sum investment of £100. For example, an annuity rate of 16.57% would mean that in return for a lump sum investment of £10,000 you would receive an annual income of 16.57% of this amount or £1,657 per annum.

Annuity rates will vary depending on the type of annuity, for example, whether it is guaranteed for five years or has no guarantee at all, whether the income is to be level or to increase at a certain rate, and on how often the income will be paid.

This table shows the *current* (August, 1985) annuity rates for males for various ages, together with the capital content:

Level annuities — males

	No guarantee		Guaranteed 5 years	
Current age	Annuity rate	Capital content	Annuity rate	Capital content
	%	%	%	%
55	11.88	4.55	11.77	4.53
60	12.70	5.54	12.50	5.49
65	13.87	6.91	13.49	6.78
70	15.53	8.84	14.77	8.51

Annuities increasing by 5% P.A. — Males

	No guarantee		Guaranteed 5 years	
Current age	Annuity rate	Capital content	Annuity rate	Capital content
	%	%	%	%
55	7.45	2.23	7.38	2.23
60	8.77	3.06	8.62	3.04
65	10.38	4.27	10.09	4.21
70	12.25	6.03	11.65	5.84

These figures illustrate a few points:

(1) The initial rates for an escalating or increasing annuity is lower than for a level one. Therefore the rate for a level annuity for a male aged 65 is 13.87% while a corresponding annuity increasing at the rate of 5% per annum is 10.38%.

(2) The rate for an annuity guaranteed for five years is lower than that for an unguaranteed period, as in the case of a guaranteed annuity, the Life Office knows that it will have to pay this amount for at least five years. In the case of the unguaranteed annuity, payment would cease immediately on death.

(3) Annuity rates increase in line with increasing age. This is natural as the older you become, the shorter your life expectancy also becomes. Therefore, the Life Assurance

Company estimates that it will have to pay out the annuity for a shorter period for somebody investing at age 70 than for somebody investing at age 60.

(4) The capital content, in other words, the part of the annuity which is not liable to income tax, also increases with increasing age at entry. This is so because it is calculated as the amount of money which you invest in the annuity divided by your expectation of life at that stage. For example, at age 65, your expectation of life might be roughly 15 years in which case the capital content, expressed as a percentage of the sum invested, works out at approximately 6⅔% per annum or 1/5th of the sum. The rationale behind this is that if you live exactly your average expectation of life from the time you take out the annuity then at the date of your death, you will have received back, free of income tax, the sum which you originally invested in the annuity.

(5) Annuity rates for females are lower than for males — in otherwords, for the same sum of money the annuity payable would be less for a female than for a male. Again, this is reasonable due to the fact that on average women live longer than men so that the life office can expect to pay out the annuity for a longer period of time.

An example will show how annuity rates work.

Let us assume that you have retired at age 65 and that you wish to purchase an annuity with a lump sum of £5,000. If you decided to purchase an annuity, with a minimum guaranteed payment period of five years, and escalating at the rate of 5% per annum compound then your yearly annuity would be as follows:-

£5,000 x 10.09% = £504.50 p.a.

Capital Content

£5,000 x 4.21% = £210.20

Therefore, you will receive a regular income of £504.50 per annum of which £210.20 per annum will be free of tax. Both the income and the capital content part will increase at the rate of 5% per annum compound. Tax at 35% on the taxable part — i.e. (£504.50 - £210.50) — would normally be deducted at source by the Life Office. If you are a higher rate taxpayer, then you must account for the balance of tax due direct to your Inspector of Taxes when you are settling up your tax affairs at the end of the year. If you are a non-tax-payer, then you can reclaim this tax deducted.

20.5 ADVANTAGES OF PURCHASED LIFE ANNUITIES

Purchased Life Annuities have fallen out of favour over the last number of years. However, they do maintain some advantages — particularly in times of very high "real" interest rates.

Such an annuity could boost your existing Pension entitlement at retirement and it does have the big advantage of certainty. When you purchase your annuity, you know exactly what level of income you will be receiving in the future. There is also the advantage that part of the income is not liable to tax.

20.6 DISADVANTAGES OF PURCHASED LIFE ANNUITIES

Perhaps the two major disadvantages of these types of annuites are as follows:-

(1) *Loss of Access to Capital:*

The purchase of an annuity is often looked on by people as involving a permanent loss of your capital. This by and large is true in that your capital has been exchanged for a guaranteed level of income in the future. It is possible to buy a "capital protected" annuity whereby on death the difference between the sum invested in the annuity and the total annuity payments to date would be returned to your estate.

However, the major disadvantage is the lack of access to your capital during your lifetime in the event of some emergency.

(2) *Uncertainty:*

Because you don't know how long you are going to live, buying an annuity involves a gamble. If you invest in an annuity and die shortly afterwards, your dependants may suffer a serious financial loss due to the loss of the capital sum invested.

(3) *Inflation:*

The purchase of a level annuity offers no protection against inflation. With an average inflation rate of 10% per annum, money halves in real value every seven years. However, you can purchase annuities with guaranteed escalation rates of up to 7½% per annum compound. As the table earlier shows there is a sharp fall in the initial level of income over a level annuity if you do purchase an escalating one.

In response to the desire for the attractions of a guaranteed level of income without the disadvantage of a permanent loss of capital, the Life Offices brought forward Guaranteed Income Bonds in recent years. These are discussed in more detail in the next Chapter.

21. GUARANTEED INCOME BONDS

21.1 GUARANTEED INCOME BONDS

Guaranteed Income Bonds, which are operated by Life Assurance Companies, have become very popular in recent years.

Guaranteed Income Bonds offer the private Investor the following attractions:

(1) A guaranteed level of income for the period of the Bond.

(2) A high net return as most of the income is *not* liable to income tax.

(3) A guaranteed return of your capital sum invested at the end of the term.

Bonds are issued for terms from two years up to ten years. The most popular terms are three and five years.

21.2 RETURNS

The rate of return offered by Guaranteed Income Bonds varies from time to time in line with fluctuating interest rates. However, once you purchase your Income Bond, your level of income is then guaranteed at the rate ruling on the date of your investment.

Currently (August, 1985) Income Bond rates are offering a gross return in the region of 8.2% for a three year Bond. The net return varies with age, sex, and your tax rate, but would be in the region of 8.2% per annum if you are taxed at 35% or approximately 8.2% if you are taxed at 60%.

Therefore, it is obvious that the difference between the gross return and net return is very small due to the fact that most of the "income" from the Bond is not in fact treated as taxable income.

21.3 HOW GUARANTEED INCOME BONDS WORK

If you invest, say, £10,000 in a three year Guaranteed Income Bond in effect you purchase two separate Annuity Contracts — one an immediate annuity and the other a deferred annuity.

Let us take an example of the £10,000 investment and assuming that you are aged 55 then the figures would work out as follows:-

Immediate Temporary Annuity:

Of your £10,000, £4,093 is allocated currently (August, 1985) to purchase an "Immediate Temporary Annuity" which will provide a gross income of £865 per annum for the next five years.

As far as income tax is concerned, the figures work out as follows:

Gross Annual Income	=	£865.00
Capital Content	=	£821.60
Taxable income	=	£ 43.40 p.a.

The income would be paid, usually half-yearly in arrear. You would only be liable to tax in respect of the taxable part that is, in this example, £43.40 per annum or less than 5% of the total income received each year.

Tax at 35% would be deducted by the Life Assurance Company at source in respect of the taxable. If your marginal rate of tax for the year is in excess of 35% then you must make up the difference with the Revenue yourself. If you are a non-taxpayer, then you can recover this tax deducted.

Deferred Annuity with Cash Option:

The balance of the £10,000 investment, that is £5,907 is used to purchase a deferred annuity. A deferred annuity is an annuity which commences at the end of a certain period — in this case at the end of the three year term of the Bond.

However, this figure is really a notional one as the deferred annuity carries a guaranteed cash option, in lieu of the annuity, of £10,000.

The net effect of this is that the deferred annuity part of the Income Bond guarantees to return your full original sum invested at the end three years.

21.4 ADVANTAGES OF GUARANTEED INCOME BONDS

Income Bonds have become very popular outlets for lump sum investment in recent years. The main advantages to the private Investor are:-

(1) They currently provide a high guaranteed "real" level of income for the chosen term.

The returns which the Life Office can offer on Income Bonds are closely related to the returns which they in turn can obtain on short-dated Government Securities. In recent years the yields on these securities have been at an historic high in "real" terms, that is after allowing for inflation. For example, *currently* gilts are yielding in the region of 10.5% per annum for short term stock compared with an inflation rate in the region of 5% per annum. Because of complicated tax reasons, the Life Assurance Company can afford to pass back most of this gross return direct to the Investor.

(2) There is little or no tax liability on the investment return.

In the example earlier less than 2% of the annual income is actually treated as taxable income.

(3) Income Bonds offer a guaranteed return of your lump sum investment at the end of the term.

Income Bonds are a particularly attractive way of providing a high level of income for higher rate tax payers, particularly higher rate taxpayers.

21.5 SOME DRAWBACKS

There are a few points which the Investor should bear in mind when looking at Guaranteed Income Bonds:-

(1) Once you purchase your Income Bond, the return is fixed for the term. Therefore the timing of purchase is crucial. The level of income provided by the Income bond remains level throughout the chosen term.

(2) Income Bonds tie-up your money for the period of the Bond. If you surrender your Income Bond before the maturity date there may be a capital loss.

(3) When your Bond matures, you may only be able to reinvest the lump sum to obtain a lower rate of return. For example, if you had invested in a Guaranteed Income Bond a few years ago and obtained a 15% p.a. return, you could now reinvest the lump sum to obtain, perhaps, just a 10½% return. Also the lump sum has not been increased to take account of inflation.

22. INVESTING A LUMP SUM

22.1 OTHER INVESTMENT OUTLETS

There are other investment outlets where you could consider investing part or all of any additional capital sums which you have put aside for your retirement. It is obviously beyond the scope of this book to go into this area in detail. However, we outline some of the main points which apply to each of the areas covered here.

22.2 UNIT-LINKED INVESTMENT BONDS

Unit-Linked Investment Bonds are operated by Life Assurance Companies. You invest a capital sum to purchase units in a Unit Fund operated by the Company. All investment income and capital gains and losses are rolled up within the Fund, less certain tax charges applicable to the Life Assurance Company, so that the value of the units as published regularly in the newspapers fully reflects the investment profits and losses to date.

There is often an "automatic income" facility attaching to these Unit-Linked Bonds. For example, some Companies will allow you to withdraw on a regular basis either a fixed monetary amount per annum or a certain proportion of the units. For example, you might be able to encash each year 10% of the units attaching to your Bond.

However, it is important to realise that you are not drawing "income" from your investment. You are in effect making a partial encashment or withdrawal of your capital invested so that if unit values are not increasing by at least the rate at which you are encashing them, then you are eating into your capital sum to provide an income. There is not necessarily anything wrong with this provided you realise that this is what is happening. Therefore, the "automatic income" feature of Unit-Linked Bonds should be used with caution. For example, if you are withdrawing 10% of your units each year but unit values are growing at just 5% per annum, then you are eating further and further into your capital sum invested.

Unit-Linked Investment Bonds are risk investments — depending on the choice of Fund, the value of the units are not guaranteed and may fluctuate in line with investment markets generally.

From a taxation point of view, the individual investor has no personal tax liability — all income and capital gains tax liabilities are discharged within the Fund and the value of the units reflects the deductions made for tax liabilities.

22.3 INDEX LINKED SAVINGS BONDS

Index Linked Savings Bonds are a Government guaranteed investment operated by An Post. They are now available for any individual from age 7 upwards subject to a maximum holding of £15,000 per person.

As the name implies, Index Linked Savings Bonds guarantee to increase the value of your investment in line with inflation for at least three years. In addition, at the end of the three year period there is an additional fixed bonus of 5% of your original investment sum payable.

Where inflation falls to low levels, as at present, there is a minimum guaranteed rate of return which works out at approximately 7¾% per annum. All returns under the Index Linked Savings Bonds are free of tax.

These Bonds can be purchased in units of £50 so that as far as providing an income for yourself is concerned, you could invest a lump sum and encash part of your investment in small amounts on a regular basis to provide a tax free income.

However, *currently* (August, 1985) Index Linked Savings Bonds do not look particularly attractive as the minimum guaranteed return of approximately 7¾% per annum can be easily bettered by, for example, a Guaranteed Income Bond or Savings Certificates. However, if the rate of inflation were to increase sharply, then

Index Linked Savings Bonds might regain the attraction which they had a number of years ago.

22.4 SAVINGS CERTIFICATES

The tenth issue of Savings Certificates which is currently available offers a guaranteed, tax free, return over five years of 10% per annum. For every £1,000 you invest, you are guaranteed to receive £1,610 after five years. However, there is also guaranteed early encashment terms before five years which work out at approximately 8% per annum. The guaranteed encashment values and the equivalent annualised rates of return are set out in this table:

Certificate encashed after years	Encashment value per £1,000 investment £	Equivalent annual rate of return % p.a.
½	1,040	8.2
1	1,085	8.5
1½	1,130	8.4
2	1,185	8.8
2½	1,240	8.9
3	1,304	9.2
3½	1,369	9.3
4	1,444	9.6
4½	1,524	9.8
5	1,610	10.0

You could therefore purchase Savings Certificates and encash them at regular intervals before the five year maturity to produce the types of returns shown in the Table above. The maximum holding is £25,000 per person.

22.5 GOVERNMENT SECURITIES

There is a wide range of Government Securities which give a guaranteed level of income plus a capital maturity value over various terms.

Government Securities range in term from stocks which mature within a matter of months to stocks which have a maturity date twenty years on. Some stocks carry low coupon rates while others carry higher rates. The coupon rate is the level of income per £100 nominal value stock which the Government will pay out each year until the stock matures. The longer the term of stock and the lower the coupon rate, the more volatile the market value of the stock becomes.

The main disadvantage of Government Securities from the private investors' point of view is that all income received from them is fully liable to income tax. Therefore, for a high rate tax-payer, this tends to make high coupon Government Securities unattractive. On the other hand, low coupon stocks may be attractive to a high rate tax-payer, but only in respect of the capital gain which can be made by holding the stock to maturity. Any capital gain on Government Securities is tax-free.

As a means of providing a regular income, Government Stocks would be suitable mainly to non-tax payers or to people paying tax at standard rate only.

An example of the type of stock which is available is the 10% Capital which matures on the 15th May, 1989.

£1000 nominal value of this stock can *currently* (August, 1985) be bought for approximately £986.00.

This would provide an income of £100 per annum payable half-yearly up until and including the 15th May, 1989 when £1000 would be repaid. The income yield on your investment is therefore in the region of 10.1% per annum which, allowing for tax at 35%, would be a net guaranteed yield of 6.6% per annum for the next five years. On maturity on the 15th May, 1989, there would be a capital profit of £14.00 on top of the return of the original £986.00 invested. However, in the intervening five-year period, the market value of the stock could fluctuate in line with interest rate movements although the value will obviously move towards the £1000 maturity value in five years time.

High coupon Securities may be suitable for non-taxpayers and basic rate taxpayers who want a guaranteed return plus access to their capital in the case of emergency, and who are prepared to accept some degree of risk until the stock matures.

22.6 UNIT TRUSTS

There is often some confusion between Unit Trusts and Unit-Linked Investment Bonds.

There are some Unit Trusts available to private investors. These Unit Trusts are not linked directly to Life Assurance Companies. If you invest money in these Unit Trusts you will receive income distributions every six months. These income dividends will have tax deducted at source at the rate of 35% but you are liable for any higher rate tax liability, depending on your tax status. In addition, the value of units will fluctuate in line with the underlying asset values.

Unit Trusts are therefore fundamentally different from Unit-Linked Investment Bonds, as far as the private Investor is concerned, because under Unit Trusts, the income which you receive is liable to tax. The capital value of your units is not being encroached on to pay the income. Of course the value of your capital units will fluctuate in line with the capital value of the underlying securities.

A high yielding Unit Trust can offer an attractive balance between a regular income plus the prospect of some capital appreciation. However, the income level will vary in line with the level of investment return which the Unit Trust can obtain on its investments. However, for a high rate tax payer, in particular, investing in a Unit Trust to provide income is not very tax efficient.

22.7 BUILDING SOCIETY DEPOSIT

Building Society Deposits have traditionally been the haven for lump sum investments for people in retirement. A Building Society Deposit is perceived as being totally capital secure plus earning an attractive rate of interest.

Building Society investment rates are net of tax at 35%. If you are a non-tax payer there is no provision whereby you can reclaim this tax deducted at source. For high rate tax-payers there is an additional tax liability representing the difference between your marginal rate of tax and the standard rate of tax.

For example, *currently* Building Society investment rates are in the region of 6.75% per annum. This rate is net of 35% tax. If your marginal rate of tax is 48% then you would have an additional tax liability of (48% — 35%) x 7.25% = .87% so that your net return becomes 5.87% per annum. The corresponding net figure for a 60% taxpayer is 5.0% per annum.

Many Building Societies now operate monthly income schemes whereby your investment income is paid on a monthly basis by cheque. However, it should be remembered that the level of your income will fluctuate in line with the fluctuating Building Society investment rate and that if you are other than a standard rate taxpayer, you will have an additional liability.

It should also be remembered that while your capital is "secure" in the sense that its value is not fluctuating as with, for example, a Unit-Linked Investment Bond, its "real" value will be steadily declining with inflation each year.

22.8 BANK DEPOSITS

The banks can really be split into three separate categories — the Associated Banks, the non-Associated Banks, and the Trustee Savings Bank.

Associated Banks:

A deposit in the Associated Banks would currently be earning a return in the region of 6% per annum before tax. All investment income from a bank deposit is liable to tax but there is a threshold below which tax is not liable. The limit on interest for tax purposes for 1985/86 is £50.00 for an individual and £100.00 for a married couple. These limits are doubled for people aged 65 years or over. These limits apply to the total interest received from all the banks including the non-Associated Banks.

Non-Associated Banks:

Non-Associated Banks would include the merchant banks and various finance houses who accept deposits from the public. Generally speaking their rates of interest are much higher than the rates offered by the Associated Banks but they also usually insist on a much higher minimum deposit, sometimes as high as £10,000. Some of these banks operate monthly income schemes whereby interest is paid monthly by cheque or credit transfer to your bank account. All interest is liable to tax without any limit except in the case of Ansbacher & Company Limited, Barclays Commercial Bank Ltd., Guinness+Mahon Limited, Chase Bank (Ireland) Limited and the Agricultural Credit Corporation Limited where the £50.00 and £100.00 exemption limits referred to above apply. However, these exemption limits apply to the total of all interest received from all bank deposits.

Trustee Savings Bank:

The Trustee Savings Bank operates an investment account, with one months notice of withdrawal, which *currently* (August, 1985) pays a rate of 11¼% per annum. The minimum deposit is £1,000 The big advantage of this particular deposit rate is that the interest exemption limit for income tax purposes is £120.00 for an individual and £240 for a married couple. These limits are *doubled* for persons aged 65 years of age or over so that, for example, for a married couple both over age 65, the total interest which could be earned from the Trustee Savings Bank free of tax would be £480 in a year.

Appendices

APPENDIX I

CIVIL SERVICE PENSIONS

PURCHASING ADDED YEARS BY PERIODICAL CONTRIBUTIONS

For an officer whose minimum retiring age is 60, and who opts to buy notional service by periodical deductions from salary, the following table shows the rate of contribution (as a percentage of salary) for each year of notional service which will be levied on salary payable between the date of the officer's next birthday and the date on which he attains minimum retiring age:

Age next birthday at exercise of option	Contribution for women	Contribution for men who are members of the civil service widows' & children's pension scheme	Contribution for men who are not members of the widows' & children's pension scheme
	%	%	%
20	.21	.23	.16
21	.22	.24	.17
22	.23	.27	.19
23	.24	.28	.20
24	.26	.30	.22
25	.28	.32	.24
26	.30	.34	.25
27	.32	.36	.27
28	.34	.38	.29
29	.36	.41	.31
30	.38	.42	.32
31	.40	.44	.34
32	.43	.46	.35
33	.46	.48	.37
34	.49	.51	.39
35	.53	.53	.41
36	.57	.56	.43
37	.61	.59	.46
38	.65	.63	.49
39	.68	.66	.52

Age next birthday at exercise of option	Contribution for women	Contribution for men who are members of the civil service widows' & children's pension scheme	Contribution for men who are not members of the widows' & children's pension scheme
	%	%	%
40	.73	.71	.56
41	.77	.76	.60
42	.83	.81	.64
43	.89	.88	.70
44	.95	.95	.76
45	1.04	1.03	.83
46	1.12	1.13	.92
47	1.22	1.25	1.02
48	1.34	1.36	1.12
49	1.49	1.50	1.24
50	1.66	1.69	1.41
51	1.87	1.89	1.58
52	2.12	2.14	1.80
53	2.44	2.50	2.11
54	2.95	2.97	2.52
55	3.53	3.55	3.03
56	4.49	4.61	3.95
57	6.25	6.03	5.20
58	9.00	9.39	8.14

APPENDIX II

CIVIL SERVICE PENSIONS

PURCHASING ADDED YEARS BY LUMP SUM CONTRIBUTION

For an officer whose minimum retiring age is 60, and who opts to buy notional service by a lump sum payment, the following table shows the rate of contribution for one year of notional service for each £100 of pensionable pay:

Age next birthday at exercise of option	Contribution for women	Contribution for men who are members of the civil service widows' & children's pension scheme	Contribution for men who are not members of the widows' & children's pension scheme
	£	£	£
20	7.95	9.57	6.63
21	8.07	9.60	6.72
22	8.24	9.65	6.84
23	8.40	9.76	7.01
24	8.57	9.87	7.18
25	8.72	9.97	7.34
26	8.89	10.08	7.50
27	9.05	10.20	7.66
28	9.21	10.35	7.83
29	9.37	10.50	7.99
30	9.54	10.66	8.14
31	9.76	10.85	8.31
32	10.02	11.04	8.48
33	10.25	11.23	8.64
34	10.48	11.41	8.80
35	10.70	11.59	8.96
36	10.92	11.78	9.13
37	11.15	11.95	9.29
38	11.42	12.14	9.48
39	11.63	12.37	9.71
40	11.86	12.65	9.98
41	12.09	12.88	10.20

Age next birthday at exercise of option	Contribution for women	Contribution for men who are members of the civil service widows' & children's pension scheme	Contribution for men who are not members of the widows' & children's pension scheme
	£	£	£
42	12.31	13.12	10.43
43	12.64	13.33	10.65
44	12.93	12.53	10.87
45	13.22	13.78	11.14
46	13.54	13.97	11.36
47	13.83	14.16	11.59
48	14.11	14.45	11.91
49	14.44	14.73	12.20
50	14.77	15.04	12.52
51	15.11	15.32	12.81
52	15.46	15.63	13.14
53	15,84	16.01	13.53
54	16.20	16.35	13.88
55	16.61	16.67	14.22
56	17.07	17.04	14.22
57	17.51	17.48	15.07
58	17.99	17.84	15.47
59	18.46	18.26	15.93
60	18.94	18.75	16.46
61	18.98	18.79	16.50
62	19.02	18.83	16.54
63	19.06	18.87	16.58
64	19.09	18.94	16.65
65	19.20	19.04	16.75

APPENDIX III

P.R.S.I. EMPLOYEE CONTRIBUTION RATES 1985/86

Contribution Class	First £13,000 of earnings	Earnings between £13,000 & £13,800	Earnings in excess of £13,800
	%	%	%
A1	8.5	7.5	2.0
B1	3.9	2.9	2.0
C1	3.9	2.9	2.0
D1	3.9	2.9	2.0
H1	8.4	7.4	2.0
J1	3.0	2.0	2.0
K1	3.0	2.0	2.0

Notes:

(1) The 1% income levy is included in the employee's share if the pay for any week is more than £102. The levy is not included in the employee's share if the pay for the week is £102 or less.

(2) The 2% contribution on all earnings in excess of £13,800 yearly represents the Youth Employment Levy and the Income Levy.

APPENDIX IV

RETIREMENT PENSION — CONTRIBUTION CONDITIONS

In order to qualify for Retirement Pension a Claimant

(a) Must have entered insurance before reaching age 55. Insurance which was paid prior to 1953 can be taken into account to satisfy this condition. If a Claimant first enters insurance after this age he/she is entitled to a refund of the portion of the social insurance contribution paid by him/her attributable to retirement pension.

(b) Must have at least 156 contribution weeks of insurable employment for which the appropriate contributions have been paid. Contributions paid prior to 1953 can be taken into account to satisfy this condition.

(c) Must have a yearly average of at least 24 contribution weeks registered (paid or credited) per contribution year from 1953 (of from the begining of the contribution year in which he/she entered insurance if this is later than 1953) up to the end of the contribution year before he/she reaches age 65. Contributions paid prior to 1953 *cannot* be taken into account to satisfy this condition.

Where pre-1953 insurance is taken into account to satisfy condition (a) or (b) the yearly average is calculated from 1953 up to the end of the contribution year before the Claimant reaches age 65.

APPENDIX V

INCOME TAX ALLOWANCES AND TAX BANDS 1985/86

Tax Bands	1985/86 £
A. Single & Widowed	
First	4,500 at 35%
Next	2,800 at 48%
Over	7,300 at 60%
B. MARRIED	
First	9,000 at 35%
Next	5,600 at 48%
Over	14,600 at 60%

Personal Allowances	1985/86
Allowance	£
Single	1,900
Widowed	2,400
Married	3,800
PAYE	600
PRSI	286
Child	100
Incapacitated Child	600
Blind Person	600
Both Spouses Blind	1,400
Dependent Relative	110
Age — Single or Widowed	100
Married	200
Employee to take care of Incapacitated Person	2,500
One Parent Families	
— Widowed	1,400
— Other	1,900

General Income Exemption Limits

	Single 1985/86 £	Married 1985/86 £
Under 65 years	2,650	5,300
65 to 75 years	3,000	6,000
Over 75 years	3,500	7,000

APPENDIX VI

CONTRIBUTORY OLD AGE PENSION — CONTRIBUTION CONDITIONS

Contribution Conditions
In order to qualify for contributory Old Age Pension a Claimant:

(a) If born between lst April, 1919 and lst September, 1922 must have become insured before reaching age 57.

If born on or after lst October, 1922 must have become insured before reaching age 56.

Insurance which was paid prior to 1953 can be taken into account in order to satisfy this condition.

If a Claimant enters insurance for the *first* time after the prescribed age he/she is entitled to a refund of the portion of the social insurance contribution paid by him/her which is attributable to contributory Old Age Pension.

(b) Must have at least 156 contribution weeks of insurable employment for which the appropriate contributions have been paid. Insurance which was paid prior to 1953 can be taken into account in order to satisfy this condition.

(c) Must have a yearly average of at least 20 contribution weeks registered (paid or credited) per contribution year from 1953 (or from the start of the contribution year in which he entered insurance if this is later than 1953) up to the end of the contribution year before reaching age 66. Insurance which was paid prior to 1953 *cannot* be taken into account in order to satisfy this condition. If pre-1953 insurance is taken into account in order to satisfy condition (a) or (b) the yearly average will be calculated over the period from 1953 up to the end of the contribution year before reaching age 66.

APPENDIX VII

CONTRIBUTORY WIDOW'S PENSION — CONTRIBUTION CONDITIONS

The contribution conditions for widow's contributory pension may be satisfied on either the husband's or the widow's own record. Contributions after the date of the husband's death cannot be counted in determining title to this pension. There are two contribution conditions:

First Condition:
There must be at leat 156 contribution weeks of insurable employment for which the appropriate contributions have been *paid* between the date of entry into insurance and the date the husband died or reached pension age (see note 1).

Second Condition:
If four years or longer have elapsed since entry into insurance, there must be a yearly average of at least 39 contribution weeks registered (*paid* or *credited*) in either of the three or five contribution years before he died or attained pension age [see note (1)]. Alternatively, this condition may be satisfied if there is an average of at least 24 contribution weeks registered (*paid* or *credited*) since entry into insurance.

On the three or five year test, the average of 39 gives title to full pension. On the extended average test, the average of 24 gives title to the minimum pension — for full pension on the extended average test, a yearly average of 48 is required.

Notes

(1) If the widow's own insurance is to be reckoned, her insurance up to the date of her husband's death is counted or, if she attained pension age prior to that date, her insurance up to the date she attained pension age is counted. The pension age from 1st October, 1977 is 66 years.

(2) As from 1st April, 1973, insurance or employment of the deceased husband in any of the EEC countries may also be taken into account in calculating a widow's title to contributory widow's pension. Accordingly, a widow should give details of her late husband's employment in any other EEC country when claiming pension.

APPENDIX VIII

NON-CONTRIBUTORY OLD AGE PENSION — MEANS TEST

Calculation of Means

In calculating a person's yearly means account is taken of:

(a) The income which such person may reasonably expect to receive during the succeeding year in cash such as earnings or allowances. (Account is *not* taken, however, of the items listed below.)

(b) The yearly value of any property belonging to but not personally used by the Claimant, such as money in bank. The rule of calculating the yearly value of such property is as follows:-
 (1) The first £200 is excluded.
 (2) The next £375 is calculated at 5%.
 (3) Any excess over £575 is calculated at 10%.

 If the weekly value (the yearly value divided by 52) of any such property is calculated at £1 or more the weekly means are taken to be the weekly value plus £1.

(c) The yearly value of any advantage accruing to the person from the use or enjoyment of property (other than furniture or personal effects), which is personally used or enjoyed by him or her, such as a farm, but excluding a domestic dwelling or a farm building owned and occupied or a vested cottage provided under the Labourers' Acts so long as payment for the purchase annuity has not been completed.

Items Excluded in Calculating Means

No account is taken of the following items in arriving at the amount of cash income which is reckoned as means:-

(i) Supplementary Welfare Allowance paid by a local authority or health board.

(ii) Income from investment or profitable use of property, not being property personally used or enjoyed by that person (but see (b) above as to the method of assessment of the capital value of the property.)

(iii) Any sums received by way of pension, allowance, assistance or benefit under the Old Age Pensions Acts, the Unemployment Assistance Acts, the Widows' and Orphans' Pensions Acts, the Children's Allowances Acts, or the Social Welfare Acts.

(iv) Any income arising from a bonus under a schedule administered by the Minister for the Gaeltacht for the making of special grants to parents or guardians resident in the Gaeltacht or Breac-Ghaeltacht of children attending primary schools.

(v) (a) Any income from a charitable organisation being a body whose activities are carried on otherwise than for profit (but excluding any public or local authority) and one of whose functions is to assist persons in need by making grants of money to them, and

(b) any income (other than income of the kind specified in Clause (a) of this sub-paragraph) from voluntary or gratuitous payments in so far as it does not exceed £52.25 per year.

(vi) Allowances paid by a local authority under the Health Act, 1947, to persons suffering from certain infectious diseases or, under the Health Act, 1953, to certain disabled persons.

(vii) Any allowance, special allowance, dependant's allowance, disability pension or wound pension under the Army Pensions Acts, 1932 to 1973, or pension under the Military Service (Pensions) Acts, 1924 to 1964 arising out of service in the period 23rd April, 1916 to 3oth September, 1923, or pension under the Connaught Rangers (Pensions) Acts 1936 to 1964.

(viii) Any pension or allowance under the Army Pensions Acts, 1923 to 1973 or pension under the Military Service (Pensions) Acts, 1924 or 1964 (or combination of such pensions or allowances) not arising out of service in the period 23rd April, 1916 to 30th September, 1923, except so far as the amount exceeds £80 (a British war pension is treated in this respect as if it were a pension or allowance under the Army Pensions Acts).

(ix) In the case of a blind person his or her earnings up to a limit of £312 increased by £208 if the person has a dependant wife or husband and by £104 in respect of each qualified child: if the blind person is a widower or a single man and is wholly or mainly maintaining a female person over the age of sixteen years for the purpose of having the care of one of more qualified children, up to £208 of his earnings are excluded (as in the case of a dependant wife) in respect of her.

(x) Any income arising from a grant or allowance given by a local authority under the Blind Persons Act, 1920.

(xi) Where the claimant is a husband separated from his wife, any payments made by him to her under a separation order.

(xii) Earnings of handicapped persons from work performed at home on materials supplied under schemes that are, in the opinion of the Minister for Social Welfare, charitable in character and purpose, so far as they do not exceed £52 a year.

(xiii) In the case of a person who is not a blind person and who has a qualified child or qualified children his or her earnings up to a limit of £104 in respect of each qualified child.

(xiv) Any income by way of annuity under Section 6 of the Land Act, 1965 except in so far as it exceeds £156 per annum.

(xv) Any moneys in respect of redundancy or change of residence paid under a statutory scheme administered by the Minister for Labour.

Means of Married Couples

In calculating the means of a person who is one of a married couple living together, the means are taken to be one-half of the total means of the couple.

Transfers of Property etc. ignored in certain cases

If a person transfers property or income for the sole purpose of qualifying for a pension, the transfer is ignored in calculating his means for pension purposes save in the case of the assignment of a farm to a child or children of the assignor, where the rateable value, including buildings, does not exceed £30 (and provided that the assignor has not been owner or occupier of lands exceeding that value in the three years preceding the date of the relevant claim to pension or application for increase of pension).

Notification of Increase of Means

A person who is in receipt of a pension or who is claiming a pension must notify any increase in income or property within three months from the end of the month in which the increase occurs.

APPENDIX IX

NON-CONTRIBUTORY OLD AGE PENSION — BENEFIT RATES

Where weekly means as assessed are	Rate per week £	Increase per week for adult dependant £
Up to £ 6.00	44.00	22.10
Over £ 6.00 and up to £ 8.00	42.00	21.10
Over £ 8.00 and up to £10.00	40.00	20.10
Over £10.00 and up to £12.00	38.00	19.10
Over £12.00 and up to £14.00	36.00	18.10
Over £14.00 and up to £16.00	34.00	17.10
Over £16.00 and up to £18.00	32.00	16.10
Over £18.00 and up to £20.00	30.00	15.10
Over £20.00 and up to £22.00	28.00	14.10
Over £22.00 and up to £24.00	26.00	13.10
Over £24.00 and up to £26.00	24.00	12.10
Over £26.00 and up to £28.00	22.00	11.10
Over £28.00 and up to £30.00	20.00	10.10
Over £30.00 and up to £32.00	18.00	9.10
Over £32.00 and up to £34.00	16.00	8.10
Over £34.00 and up to £36.00	14.00	7.10
Over £36.00 and up to £38.00	12.00	6.10
Over £38.00 and up to £40.00	10.00	5.10
Over £40.00 and up to £42.00	8.00	4.10
Over £42.00 and up to £44.00	6.00	3.10
Over £44.00 and up to £46.00	4.00	2.10
Over £46.00 and up to £48.00	2.00	1.10
Over £48.00	Nil	Nil

Note
Depending on the amount of his/her weekly means in excess of £48.00 a Pensioner with children may receive a reduced pension.

Increases to above

Increases for Children:	Rate per week
First child	£ 9.30
Second Child	£10.50
Third to Fifth Child	£ 8.15
Sixth and subsequent Children	£ 6.50

Living alone allowance for Pensioner over 66	£ 3.40
Extra allowance for Pensioner aged 80 and over	£ 3.20

APPENDIX X

NON-CONTRIBUTORY WIDOW'S PENSION — BENEFIT RATES

Where weekly means as assessed are	Rate per week beneficiary under 66 £	Rate per week beneficiary over 66 £
Up to £ 6.00	43.15	44.00
Over £ 6.00 and up to £ 8.00	41.15	42.00
Over £ 8.00 and up to £10.00	39.15	40.00
Over £10.00 and up to £12.00	37.15	38.00
Over £12.00 and up to £14.00	35.15	36.00
Over £14.00 and up to £16.00	33.15	34.00
Over £16.00 and up to £18.00	31.15	32.00
Over £18.00 and up to £20.00	29.15	30.00
Over £20.00 and up to £22.00	27.15	28.00
Over £22.00 and up to £24.00	25.15	26.00
Over £24.00 and up to £26.00	23.15	24.00
Over £26.00 and up to £28.00	21.15	22.00
Over £28.00 and up to £30.00	19.15	20.00
Over £30.00 and up to £32.00	17.15	18.00
Over £32.00 and up to £34.00	15.15	16.00
Over £34.00 and up to £36.00	13.15	14.00
Over £36.00 and up to £38.00	11.15	12.00
Over £38.00 and up to £40.00	9.15	10.00
Over £40.00 and up to £42.00	7.15	8.00
Over £42.00 and up to £44.00	5.15	6.00
Over £44.00 and up to £46.00	3.15	4.00
Over £46.00 and up to £48.00	Nil	2.00
Over £48.00	Nil	Nil

Note
Depending on the amount of her weekly means in excess of £46.00 a Pensioner with children may receive a reduced pension.

Increases to above

	Rate per week under 66	Rate per week over 66
Increases for Children:		
First child	£11.25	£11.50
Second to Fifth Child	£12.35	£12.65
Sixth and subsequent children	£10.60	£10.80
Living alone allowance for Pensioner over 66		£ 3.40
Extra allowance for Pensioner aged 80 and over		£ 3.20

APPENDIX XI

NON-CONTRIBUTORY ORPHAN'S PENSION — BENEFIT RATES

Where the weekly means as assessed are:	Rate per week orphan £
Up to £ 1.00	24.50
Over £ 1.00 and up to £ 3.00	22.50
Over £ 3.00 and up to £ 5.00	20.50
Over £ 5.00 and up to £ 7.00	18.50
Over £ 7.00 and up to £ 9.00	16.50
Over £ 9.00 and up to £11.00	14.50
Over £11.00 and up to £13.00	12.50
Over £13.00 and up to £15.00	10.50
Over £15.00 and up to £17.00	8.50
Over £17.00 and up to £19.00	6.50
Over £19.00 and up to £21.00	4.50
Over £21.00 and up to £23.00	2.50
Over £23.00	Nil